Letters from Rome

During Vatican II

ALOYSIUS J. WYCISLO

Paisa Publishing Co.
De Pere, Wisconsin

Cover picture: Opening session of the Second Vatican Council, in St. Peter's Basilica in Rome.

Cover design: Douglas Hjorth

Acknowledgements

To Bishop Robert Morneau for editing the original manuscript, Sisters Clarita Ryan OSF and Jacquiline Koenig OSF for correcting secretarial mistakes and several friends who after reading the manuscript of letters urged its publication.

The daily summaries in English of the Council sessions provided by and for the American Bishops in Rome were an invaluable source of information for these letters to the parishioners of the Immaculate Heart of Mary Parish in Chicago.

Printed in the United States of America
Library of Congress Control Number: 2005909299
ISBN 0-9764782-2-6

Paisa Publishing Co.
(Alt Publishing Co.)
502 George Street
De Pere, WI 54115
(920) 983-5326

In Memoriam

Most Rev. Aloysius J. Wycislo

June 17, 1908 - October 11, 2005

"For anyone born after Vatican II it could be difficult to appreciate how challenging the conciliar emphasis on 'being church' – that is, on being the 'people of God' – is"

(Regis Duffy)

Contents

Introduction

After sixteen years in pioneering the work of Catholic Relief Services, the international charitable agency of the American Catholic Hierarchy, I returned to Chicago to become one of the auxiliary bishops to his Eminence Albert Cardinal Meyer. I was also asked to take on the responsibilities of a parish. The parish was a vibrant community of some two thousand families with several assistant priests. As an auxiliary bishop I was necessarily away from the parish on most weekends, and several months of the year during the four sessions of the Second Vatican Council II.

As a consequence, and in order to keep in touch with my parishioners, I wrote a weekly article for the parish bulletin and did so during the sessions of the Council from Rome. Interestingly, the letters became sought-after amplification of news from the Vatican Council not often covered in the local press.

In between sessions of the Council there was the inevitable homework we bishops received from Rome. Not only was there new material that needed to be studied for future discussion, but further augmentation of the schema or documents Council committees had been working on. I not only continued to use the parish bulletin to keep my parishioners informed about the Council but included implication of how the Council documents might affect their religious lives and practices.

In the ensuing years, especially after I became the bishop of the Diocese of Green Bay, Wisconsin in 1968, I used many of those letters from Rome as background for the lectures I was asked to give on the Second Vatican Council.

Many times some listeners to those lectures would tell me that I made the documents of the Council come alive, and some said, "Why don't you make those letters available to a wider genera-tion of people living out the consequences of the Council with little understanding of its background and history."

Those remarks moved me to search out my files on Vatican II. I so enjoyed re-reading those files and those letters I wrote from Rome between 1962 and 1965 that indeed, I felt that the publishing of those letters would not only provide deeper insight on my first book on the Council, *Vatican II Revisited*, (Alba House, New York, 1987), but opportunity for a post-Vatican II generation to learn the origins and reasons of the why and how of the faith they practice today.

Therefore, I bring together a re-telling, for your enjoyment and learning, not the dry bones and records of Vatican II, but that human dimension of the two Popes, more than two thousand bishops, several hundred "periti" or experts, and other Christian observers, who provided us with the seed-bed for the renewal of our Church perhaps for centuries to come.

Bishop Wycislo

Leaving for Rome

September 24, 1962 - October 10, 1962

September 24, 1962

When you read this, I will be at sea on the U.S. liner Constitution, sailing for Rome and the October 11th opening of the Second Vatican Council. I am in the good company of our Cardinal Archbishop Meyer, Bishop Hillinger, Bishop O'Donnell, and the Cardinal's secretary, Msgr. Clifford Bergin. On the ship are other prelates from other parts of our country whom you probably would not know.

Please keep us in your prayers as we carry to Rome, to that great gathering of bishops from all parts of the world, your needs and the needs of our parish and of our archdiocese. You are all close to my heart and I am grateful for this means of keeping in touch with you. You too are in my prayers and especially in the Masses that I offer for your intentions.

For the next few months I will write to you as often as I can with the hope that our parish priests will be able to find room in the parish bulletin for some parts of my letters. Some may be too long for the allotted space and so I leave that to their judgment. I promise to tell you everything about Rome and the meetings that we will be having there. So it is that you have your own exclusive reporter on the events of the forthcoming Council of Vatican II.

I leave the parish in the hands of the Immaculate Heart of our Lady whose title we honor and the very capable hands of my brother priests. Help them as you have helped me. They too, are devoted to your needs. Make their burdens light, their worries few and help them pay the bills. By the way, I am asking them to conduct a novena in preparation for the Ecumenical Council of Vatican II. Be sure to attend that novena and pray for the success of the Council and for all the bishops who will soon be converging on the Eternal City.

The captain of the Constitution told us at dinner last night that it will be another three days before we dock in Naples, Italy. Before we do, two stops are planned, one at the island of Malta and the other at Palermo, on the island of Sicily.

Early this morning we sighted the island of Malta and soon after breakfast we were invited to tour the island, at least those of us who were brave enough to get into a small boat for the half hour trip to the dock. Malta is just fifty-eight miles south of the island of Sicily, which we will reach sometime tomorrow. The island seems to lie in the central Mediterranean Sea about halfway between Italy and North Africa. As a matter of fact, when we landed on the island we immediately noticed the influence of Moorish architecture that came from Africa and, of course, the innumerable monkeys that invade the island. You practically have to be a monkey to navigate the steep walks and by-ways that are typical of Malta.

What is even more interesting is the fact that after a shipwreck St. Paul landed on Malta and founded the Church there in A.D. 60. We were surprised to learn from the Archbishop of Valetta, the capital of the island, that there were some three hundred thousand Catholics on the island, served by 914 priests in just forty-nine parishes, and 1470 nuns in ninety-six convents looking after some 14,500 pupils in their schools. We have many dioceses in our country with as many Catholics but with just a fraction of that personnel.

Back on the U.S. Constitution there was the usual

scrumptious dinner awaiting us. Tired and grateful for the opportunity to stretch our legs after all those days at sea, and what with all that climbing on the island, it was early to bed for many of us.

This is being written after a long and interesting afternoon in Palermo on the island of Sicily. We accompanied Cardinal Meyer in a visit with his former classmate, Cardinal Ruffini in his "pallazo," in the center of the city. The "pallazo," or palace, was a huge complex of buildings with the Cathedral at the center, the Cardinal's residence to one side and his administrative or chancery offices on the other; all of that enclosed within an exquisitely walled-in garden.

But note this contrast with Malta; 1,117 priests and 3,143 nuns serving a million and a quarter Catholics in an area of 541 square miles compared to Malta's 95 square miles. The Archdiocese of Chicago comprises 1,411 square miles in which two and a quarter million Catholics are served by approximately 2,800 priests, and I would estimate at this distance, 8,500 nuns and about 450 parishes.

We were up at the break of dawn on October 4th. Our ship had docked sometime during the night in the Port of Naples. After a quick breakfast and the closing of suitcases we were down the gangplank; there to be greeted by Msgr. Joseph Howard, the Rector of our Chicago House of Studies in Rome and several other priests, among them an old friend, Msgr. Andrew Landi, with whom I lived and worked during the war years in Italy. The three-hour drive to Rome over a new and magnificent expressway was a surprise from what I remembered of the Italy I left twelve years before.

So too, the Chicago House of Studies on Via Sardegna, which was to be our home for the next several months. I remembered the high wall and pink-stuccoed building that was empty because of the war, now renovated and bursting with hospitality – several students from home; Msgr.

Marcinkus, a Chicago priest attached to the Vatican's diplomatic corps, Bishop Primeau, another Chicagoan, once Rector of the House of Studies but now the Bishop of Manchester in New Hampshire, all made us welcome.

And the staff that cooked and cleaned looked after our needs. The first of that staff I met was Renato who took me up the three flights of marble stairs to my room and suggested that I leave unpacking for the afternoon. And the late afternoon it was, what with wine at lunch, something I had to get used to, and Renato's parting phrase before I climbed those stairs again: "Buono reposo." Have a good nap!

The other people that make up the staff of our temporary home are Vera, the housekeeper and quite a lady, very proper, always dressed in grey, a native Roman who speaks exquisite Italian. Renato, whom you met earlier waits on table and is a kind of butler for all of us. There is Maria, the maid who makes our beds and tidies our rooms and sees to the laundry. And Georgio, the cook. If the lunch we had upon our arrival is any indication of the future, I'm afraid you will be welcoming back a heavier bishop.

October 7, 1962

Now that I was unpacked I was anxious to get outside for a walk to savor again what I remembered of Rome. Via Sardegna leads toward the Via Venetto, a busy thorough-fare crammed with exclusive shops and comfortable hotels. At the intersection is a newsstand where I found European editions of the *New York Times* and the *New York Herald Tribune,* as also the *Stars and Stripes,* a tabloid-sized paper that circulated among the U.S. troops occupying post -war Europe. Just down the street is the world headquarters of the Franciscan Monks; the Maryknoll Fathers have their headquarters across the street and at the corner of our street and Via Pompeii is a charming little church where bells woke us up in the morning.

What a change from the Rome I knew during the years of the war. Then, I remembered, the shops were few, with little to sell, the restaurants, non-existent; a priest friend invited me out to a kind of family restaurant with just six or eight tables. Most of the cars on the streets were drab olive-painted army vehicles and a few civilian cars belong-ing to government officials.

The contrast on this comfortably fall day in Rome was remarkable; huge buses spewing diesel exhaust fumes into the atmosphere, and hundreds of small Italian cars doing the same, scooting between and around them, miniature motorcycles, Vespas they call them, incessantly blowing their horns delayed my sleep in my room on the third floor.

Today is a quiet Sunday, just a few days before we bish-ops will be processing into the cavernous interior of St. Peter's Basilica for the opening of the Second Vatican Council. This morning, my dear parishioners, I offered Mass for your intentions. It's been such a beautiful day that soon after breakfast Msgr. Bergin and I decided on a walk. It's the best way to see and feel Rome.

Just a few streets away from our Via Sardegna, the

Borghese Gardens were already jammed with Italian families eager to get away from their cramped and noisy streets. Some were heading for the zoo at one end of the gardens, others to a miniature lake where brightly painted rental boats were at a premium. At the other end of the gardens, wealthy Romans were riding their magnificent horses along a bridle path surrounded by the famous pines of Rome. And almost at every crossroad there was a vendor dispensing "gelati" or ice cream, or even Coca-Cola and other soft drinks to parents doting over their children.

Msgr. Bergin and I made our way to the far end of the gardens toward a promontory that gave us a magnificent view of the city of Rome. Church steeples dominated our view as if pointing to the grandest of them all, the dome of St. Peter's some distance away. We turned to each other and said: "Why not, let's keep walking. The day is young." And off we went along cobbled streets until we reached the famous Via Conciliazione, the main and beautiful street leading into St. Peter's Square.

Before rushing onto the basilica we sought out a table at one of those sidewalk cafes for a "cappuccino," a delightful blend of steamed coffee and milk to pick us up for what would lie ahead. What a thrill, to be in Rome again approaching St. Peter's, the central church of our Catholic faith. The vast elliptical colonnades of Bernini, those tall columns you've seen in pictures surrounding the square that leads into St. Peter's, seemed to stretch out their arms in welcome to those who would walk the stony and worn pavement to pray and worship at the tomb of St. Peter. In a few days those same colonnades would embrace the bishops of all the world gathering for the great Council.

The early afternoon sun on this October day seemed especially benign when I think that back home the leaves in brilliant colors are already reflecting a winter's sun. As we stood there in St. Peter's Square I wondered what the fall and winter here in Rome would bring. Pope John did invite us to come and to study the "signs of the times."

We strolled past the Swiss guards into the dark interior of Christendom's most venerated church and the first thing that struck my eyes were the long tiers of seats of oak and red upholstery that would soon be filled by bishops who were told to come dressed in copes and white mitres. As I looked about the great expanse of the basilica the anticipation that gnawed at my heart and mind all those months since I received Pope John's invitation to attend the Council, now changed to awe and expectation of what was to come. Overriding all that anxiety about leaving you, making that long trip to Europe again, and the concern over the preliminary documents that were sent to me for study, was the realization of what it meant to be here in Rome, an obscure member of the apostolic hierarchy called to deliberate and maybe legislate for the Church of God.

All of a sudden I felt tired, like that feeling when anticipation becomes reality, so I turned to Msgr. Bergin and said: "Cliff, let's go back to the House." He agreed and we made our way across that bright and sunlit square to a bus, early enough for a brief nap and a light supper that followed.

The First Session
of Vatican Council II

October 11, 1962 - December 9, 1962

October 11, 1962

This was a day to remember, and before I forget, and despite the fact that I am tired and ought to be sleeping, I must share with you Pope John's dream come true, the opening day of the twenty-first Ecumenical Council, Vatican II. This was a day of ceremony as only our Church could make possible, but even more than that, a day full of hope for the Church of the future. Back home you must have watched on television what may be the most historic day of our century. Few events of a religious nature in modern times have been given the publicity that anticipated the calling of this universal meeting of the Church's hierarchy. Do you know why?

Because Pope John asked us to come together to break down the wall of isolation between the Church and the world, of eradicating distrust among us who would believe and serve our God in unity of mind and heart, of bringing our Church and each of us to an "aggiornamento," a renewal of our faith and to a dissipation of the fog of ignorance that divides those whom Christ prayed should be one.

What a resplendent scene it was this morning. I was thrilled to be a part of it. A brilliant sun warmed the procession of 2,540 cardinals, archbishops, patriarchs, and bishops as they came down the Golden Staircase of the Vatican Palace, out across St. Peter's Square into the enormous basilica of the Prince of the Apostles for the opening Mass of the Second Vatican Council.

By invitation there were seated near the main altar, close to where the ten Presidents of the Council would preside, Protestant observers who came, we hoped, to share our concern for the one Church of Christ. Later, in the Pope's homily, he stressed that at the heart of the Council was the call to unity. Some three hundred "periti," or experts in their field of learning whom the bishops and the officials of the Vatican curial offices brought to Rome to assist in developing the documents that we hoped would come out of this great gathering, and the heads of religious orders residing in Rome, watched from balconies above us.

Pope John XXIII, looking frail and aged, supported on the shoulders of six stalwart men, entered the front doors of the basilica at the end of the procession. The Pope was visibly moved by the scene in front of him. My seat, or combination desk and chair, was close to the entrance and just about a hundred feet from the back wall of St. Peter's.

The main altar seemed a mile away. The Pope asked his carriers to stop now and then along that long aisle so that he could spend a moment looking into our eyes and sharing with us the hope for success of the great work that lay ahead of us. So moving was this encounter of Pope and bishops that all along those two tiers we turned to each other to exchange a kiss of peace. The scriptural phrase ran through my mind: "How good it was for us to be here."

Mass started and there began that sense of sharing in an ultimate perfection of the liturgy as one can only witness in St. Peter's. Throughout the lofty vaults of that great basilica the voices of the Sistine Choir swelled in a mighty crescendo of the beauty of the Kyrie Eleison over the heads of the Conciliar Fathers who responded in blood-chilling response with their Kyrie Eleison, Christe Eleison. Then came the Gloria in a unison of more than three thousand voices giving glory to God in a medium of music that seemed to even please the statues of angels hanging over our heads at the end of the columns supporting the roof of St. Peter's.

In contrast came the subdued but eloquent and forceful voice of Pope John who brought us to this historic beginning of a universal council of the Church. Obviously moved, he said: "Our voice is directed to you, my venerable brothers. The longed-for day has finally dawned and we begin under the auspices of the Virgin Mother of God this Ecumenical Council. We see here with you important personalities, present in an attitude of great respect and cordial expectation, having come together in Rome from the five continents to represent the nations of the world."

"Our aim is to bring the main points and precepts of Christian doctrine to the people of God in the best possible way. But that this doctrine may influence the various fields of human activity the Church must ever look to the present, to the new conditions and the new forms of life introduced into the modern world which have opened up new avenues to the Catholic apostolate. We will need to remember that the substance of that ancient doctrine of the Deposit of Faith is one thing, and the way in which it is presented is another. Let us dedicate ourselves with an earnest will and without fear to that work which this era demands of us."

Then came the singing of the Credo in plainchant, again in the unison of several thousand voices electrifying and acknowledging the Pope's exhortation. The crowning moment came a bit later when, with the Pope, we stretched out our hands over the elements of the bread and wine that would be changed to the Body and Blood of our Lord.

It was a long morning, followed by a late lunch. I shall never get over the emotions that filled my day. With my night prayers I thought that someday on my tombstone there may be the words: "Council Father of the Church of Vatican II."

October 18, 1962

After a restful weekend following the opening day of the Second Vatican Council, we had our first working session on Monday, October 13. It was with mingled feelings of hope and expectation that we entered St. Peter's that morning. The weekend gave us an opportunity to study the rules and procedures that would govern the Council sessions. I learned that 2,908 bishops from throughout the world were eligible to be Council Fathers and that of that number, 2,540 were present at the opening sessions.

Eager to make comparisons, I found here in our library at the Chicago House of Studies a book on the First Vatican Council that opened on December 8, 1869, after "a night of heavy rain lightening and thunder." All during that summer there were efforts to continue the Council but the declaration of war between France and Prussia moved the Pope to officially suspend the Council on October 20, 1870. There were 679 bishops present at the opening of Vatican I, 40 from the United States as compared to 247 of us for the present Council. South America has the largest number of bishops here, 489, with Italy next at 430.

As I indicated earlier, Vatican II became a media event and like many of you reading the papers, we bishops kept noticing words like "progressives," "conservatives," and that stereotype that Pope John was a liberal and a reformer, that he called us to Rome to revamp the Church.

There's an element of truth in those labels. On our first working day, at least, we ran into a situation that clearly indicated the conservative stance of the curial officials in Rome, those working in the Vatican offices, and a good number of the Italian bishops who opposed the idea of a council. The first task was the reading and approval of a list of 160 bishops who would serve on the ten commissions that would examine the agenda items that were mailed to us at home. The folio-sized booklet listed names unfamiliar

At the first session of Vatican Council II, 2,540 bishops gathered at St. Peter's Basilica, with the first working session held on Monday, October 13, 1962.

to many of us. It was suggested that we take a coffee break and come back to the meeting ready to approve or disapprove of the prepared list.

Well, I had my first experience in higher Church politics. The "coffee bars" buzzed with rumor and criticism. Where did these names come from? Who proposed them? Since Cardinal Meyer was on the Preparatory Commission for the Council, Bishop O'Donnell and I sought him out for advice. He told us that the names were largely the work and inspiration of staff persons identified with the Roman Curia. His Eminence advised us to be patient and told us that one of the cardinals on his commission would be making a proposal when we returned to our places.

Apparently it was assumed by those in charge of the "housekeeping" details of the Council that the election of members-at-large for those various commissions would be a matter of routine. Doesn't that happen at our meetings at home sometimes? In any case, two cardinals, Lienart of Lille in France and Frings from Cologne in Germany, rose to speak and insisted that more thought be given to the selection of candidates for those important commissions, that the meeting be adjourned to give the various national conferences of bishops time to select and propose their candidates. The proposal was greeted with tremendous applause and the Moderator, one of the Council Presidents, had no choice but to acquiesce. And so ended our first session of Vatican II – it lasted just one hour!

Over the next few days the various national conferences of bishops met privately to discuss their position vis-a-vis membership on those commissions. In our case we from the United States met at our college in Rome on the Jeniculum, a hill overlooking St. Peter's and a section of the city of Rome. You will be interested in knowing that your bishop was chosen to serve on the Commission for Ecumenical Affairs (our relationship with other Christian Churches), the Commission on the Liturgy, a Sub-commission dealing with Indulgences, the Committee on Communications and on the Oriental Churches. The latter probably because of my contact with those churches during my years of travel for Catholic Relief Services.

After celebrating Mass with the Cardinal at our Chapel in the Chicago House and a quick breakfast, we were on our way to St. Peter's by 8:30 AM for the second session of the Council on the 16th. It was a chilly, rainy and a more typical fall day in Rome. All around me many bishops were trying to make themselves comfortable after having been caught in the rain walking across the great square into St. Peter's.

There were no cloak rooms or places to hang wet clothing. The more ingenious bishops just slung their outer gear over railings that separated the altars of saints behind the ten-tiered platforms that were our seat and desk. Others who took their wet cloaks to their places had raindrops on the papers that had accumulated there.

Our meeting began with a Mass celebrated by a bishop from Spain whose Latin accent was hard to understand. After Mass we listened patiently to Archbishop Felici, the Secretary General of the Council, who, in flawless Latin, made several announcements and cleared up the procedure of the voting schedule for the 24 offices on those ten Council commissions. Council regulations allowed us to choose sixteen bishops for each of the commissions whereas the Pope had the privilege of naming the other eight members. A bit of humor was injected into the procedure when during the coffee break rumor spread that the Italians were insisting that five members of their Episcopal conference be appointed to each of the ten commissions.

The great nave of St. Peter's became bedlam; seminarians acting as pages, began distributing all sorts of papers and booklets; a full list of Council Fathers, their addresses and telephone numbers in case we wanted to get in touch with each other, the names of consultants who served on the preparatory commissions and a book on Council rules. In any case, we cast our first ballot of the Second Vatican Council and since tabulating 2,540 ballots times 24 bishops for each of the ten commissions (that's about 500,000 names) would be quite a task, we were told that our next meeting would be on the 20th of October instead of the 17th.

October 25, 1962

Before I get into our third meeting of the Council, which was on the 20th, there is much to tell you of what went on in between. Over that long weekend I seized the opportunity to do some window shopping. It's a long walk downhill from Via Sardegna to the Piazza Minerva where I found a cluster of religious-goods shops. By chance, I wandered into the famous Gambarreli's, a haberdashery that deals exclusively with episcopal clothing and accessories. I needed a few zuchettas, that little red "beany" a bishop wears on the crown of his head. There, I ran into Cardinal Wyszynski of Poland. We embraced in usual European manner and I agreed to his invitation to dinner at his home of the following Saturday.

What a pleasant evening that was even though I stumbled through it in halting Polish, searching for words I found difficult to transfer from the English idiom that was on my mind but not on my tongue. At dinner, I met seventeen of the bishops who were able to get out of Poland to attend the Council. Three of the group I had met years before, in 1945, when I initiated relief operations for that unfortunate country.

That night back on Via Sardegna, with painstaking effort because I found it hard to sleep, I counted at least 174 cars and 30 Vespas, those miniature bikes that seem to run on a motor without a muffler. It seemed that those vehicles were going to crash into my room. How I wished that I had been given a room on the inside courtyard. It seemed to me that the Italians never go to bed.

So I picked up again that book on the history of First Vatican Council hoping to lull myself to sleep. In the 1860's, Rome had a population of some 200,000 inhabitants. Now it has more than two million, and like our big cities at home, newcomers keep pouring in from the south. Ah, but the food is great. The Roman kitchen is superb and I'm getting used to the different varieties of pasta. Veal is plentiful and prepared well. The favorite dessert is a custard with caramel sauce.

Sunday dawned beautifully and despite the disturbed night I decided on a long walk into the Villa Borghese Gardens. Going by the church around the corner from our house I was reminded of a conversation we had at dinner the other evening with one of the students at our college. He told us that thirty percent of Italian women and just ten percent of men go to church on Sunday. Back home our figures run into the eighties and seventies.

What a contrast. I thought that maybe that phrase "familiarity breeds contempt," or more politely, "disinteredness," in the Church on the part of the Italians might be a factor. On the other hand, I found Italians to be a pious and very hospitable people. So I just found myself a bench in those gardens and spent an hour watching them at play.

On the way back to Via Sardegna I picked up the English papers and while waiting for lunch, a much needed nap afterwards, I noticed reports of the Council were, to say the least, a bit garbled or even inaccurate. The media seem to want to imply that there is a pitched battle going on between the bishops and the Vatican or curial offices.

Nothing could be father from the truth. We could not get along without those offices and its dedicated members. Someone had to put together all that preparatory material for the Council, and who else but those close to Rome and the Vatican. Granted, there were some Cardinals and others who were not in favor of a Council and they told Pope John that. In a speech he gave, the Pope referred to the opposition as "prophets of doom."

Pope John must have been made aware of the garbled press coverage the Council was getting and maybe that was the reason he invited almost eight hundred news people to the beautiful Sistine Chapel for a news conference. Directing their attention to Michelangelo's great painting of the Last Judgment on the ceiling of the chapel, the Pope, with his usual charm, said to the reporters, "Be careful you do not have a great temptation. There's a bit of nudity in that painting."

But then, smiling and with outstretched arms, he said, "We felt keenly that we must meet you and tell you personally how much we desire your loyal cooperation in presenting this great event in its true colors." And then the Pope went on to urge the reporters that they not be tempted to pander to one or the other side of our debates in the Council, or be concerned with speed rather than accuracy, or even be more interested in sensationalism rather than objective truth.

I think he "hit the nail on the head" when he asked the news people not to give undue prominence to some incidental detail but to seek out the reality of the situation. He asked them not to tamper with "the most intimate and sacred matter of religion and of the soul's relationship with God."

At our third meeting of the Council on October 20th, after some discussion, the bishops decided to issue a "message to the World." Here is a short paragraph: "United here from every nation under heaven, we carry in our hearts the anxieties of all the peoples entrusted to our care, those anxieties of body and soul, all those sorrows and desires. With the help of the Holy Spirit we will seek the most effective ways of renewing ourselves and we will strive to propose to all peoples of our times the truth of God in its entirety and purity, and be always conscious of the demands of those who seek God."

On Monday the 22nd, things really got moving. As soon as the morning Mass was over, the General Secretary, Archbishop Felici, announced that twenty-one Council Fathers asked for the floor. Among them was Cardinal Spellman of New York. We were told that the document on the liturgy would be the first for discussion even though there had been some preliminary thought about the document on Revelation, dealing with the Sacred Scriptures. At dinner that evening we wondered about the switch and learned from Cardinal Meyer that since the scripture document would most surely provoke some heated debate the Presidency of the Council decided to tackle liturgy first as the most manageable document and one with which most bishops were familiar.

Now and then the debates, rather the interventions, were interrupted by the Secretary who announced the names of the bishops who had been elected to the various commissions. Also, the names of those Fathers chosen by Pope John himself were also announced. A press release I read that evening stated that 49 bishops were present from behind the Iron Curtain. Of the 64 bishops in Poland, only seventeen were allowed to come to the Council and that was true of the other countries under Communist domination. China, for instance, had no one at the Council.

October 31, 1962

There were seven meetings, or sessions as they are officially called, since I wrote to you last. Liturgy was the main topic since it is primarily concerned with the internal renewal of the Church, which, after all, is at the heart of our religion. The discussions were wide-ranging to say the least and there were some surprises. But before I get into that you should be made aware of a beautiful practice that was revised (it was done at Vatican I) as we began our daily sessions. One of the prelates flanked by two altar boys was chosen to carry the Sacred Scriptures down the aisle of St. Peter's for enthronement in front of the President's chair. Thus was the dramatic tie between worship, the Mass, and the Scriptures symbolized. I hope that practice catches on in our parishes back home.

Speakers on the liturgy emphasized the following: Local languages should be used instead of Latin in the Mass; there should be a greater variety of scriptural texts that are used in the "teaching" parts of the Mass. I suspect the latter suggestion has to do with our sermons. When one of the bishops mentioned more singing at the Mass, another objected that we were aping the Protestant churches. Communion should be received under both species – bread and wine, the Body and Blood of our Lord. When priests gather in larger numbers they should concelebrate the Mass rather than going off by themselves for a private Mass to some corner of the Church or some chapel. This would probably do away with the side altars we have in our churches today.

I should mention here that over the short time we've been in Rome we witnessed Mass in the different rites at the beginning of our sessions. The Byzantine Mass, sung in Greek and Arabic, took quite a chunk of time out of one morning's meeting. There was a liturgy according to the Melkite Rite, one of the oldest in the Church; another in the Coptic, etc. But really, these different celebrations of the one Mass made us bishops realize that while the Church is Catholic, her liturgy need not be uniform. One morning after we were discussing the funeral liturgy, a bishop from the Orient told me that black was a sign of joy for them, white, a sign of sorrow. I wonder what the color for future Masses in the United States will be like.

Language for the Mass and the sacraments became a significant issue in our discussions. A good friend, Archbishop Hallinan of Atlanta, Georgia, with whom I served on the bishops' liturgy committee, said that he was amused to hear bishops speaking in elegant Ciceronean Latin to defend the use of the vernacular in the liturgy. Seriously though, most of us here in Rome feel that the use of English in the Mass and in the sacraments would make our liturgical rites more understandable and meaningful to the faithful laity at home. I like this reasoning for the use of English in the Mass that appeared in a daily press bulletin:

> The use of the vernacular reveals the universality of Christendom, capable even in its unchangeability of assuming the values and traditions of the individual peoples, of all latitudes and all times, of the present and of the future."

The reason given for the continued use of Latin in the Mass, in that same bulletin which was quoting one of the bishops who spoke that day, went this way:

> "Latin has not only traditional values but it also has a true unifying effect. Furthermore, because of its logical precision, because of its concrete phraseology of legal terms, it is particularly suited for theology and dogma."

Would you say that this latter reason would help you participate better in the Mass? Many of the speeches I listened to these past few days stressed that because of the teaching and pastoral nature of the liturgy, the rites, that is the way we celebrate Mass and the sacraments, should be "simple, brief, easily and immediately understood." Given my pastoral experience, I agree.

There was always emphasis that the Mass is the natural center of the liturgical life of every parish. It was also repeated in many of the speeches that the laity should be given more opportunities to take an active part in the Mass and that great care and diligence should characterize preparation for the Sunday Mass.

By the way, our American bishops were holding regular meetings at the American College in the evenings on this matter of changes in the liturgy. We decided that rather than a number of us request an opportunity to speak, that one of the bishops speak for all of us, or at least for a larger number of us. Archbishop Hallinan, whom I mentioned earlier, was generally our representative on matters of the liturgy.

When all this discussion about lay participation in the liturgy came up, it also provoked some discussion about the role of women in the Church. During a coffee break one of my neighbors in what we called "the stalls," remarked "soon we'll have women dancing in the sanctuary!" Well, I thought, women are part of the laity so I said to my neighbor: "I celebrated Mass in many convents where a nun was the server, maybe women could do some of the readings even at our parish Masses."

Speaking about neighbors, I should tell you that Bishop O'Donnell and I, by reason of our being made bishops at the same time, sat next to each other. But below and behind us were bishops from Holland, England, Africa, and a delightful and entertaining bishop from Canada. Otherwise we tried to communicate in Italian or Latin. On my left was a bishop from Holland who did not understand Latin (which, by the way, was the official language of the Council) and he would frequently nudge me to ask: "What did the speaker say?" By the time I explained a bit to him, I sometimes missed a salient point in a speech.

Back to the role of women. At one of those evening meetings at the college, I ran into Martin Work, a layman who worked at our Conference headquarters in Washington. We knew each other from my frequent visits to Washington on behalf of Catholic Relief Services. Mr. Work was a prominent leader in our National Conference of Catholic Men. I mentioned my brief encounter with the bishop about the role of women in the Church. He laughed and said: "You know, Bishop, that's coming up. I was called to Rome to consult with lay leaders from other countries about lay participation in the work of the Church. By the way, an old friend of yours, Margaret Mealey, is in Rome."

Miss Mealey is the head of the National Conference of Catholic Women in the United States and a close friend of Eileen Egan, who worked with me in New York at the Catholic Relief offices. But what was interesting about that meeting with Mr. Work (and I suspect that's why Miss Mealey was in Rome) is what he said about a move to internationalize the different Catholic conferences of men and women in the world, and, the mood of Catholic women engaged in the work of those conferences who are deeply concerned about the role of women in the Church. This may surprise you, but Mr. Work also mentioned that there was talk of ordaining men to the diaconate and of dioceses having lay boards of consulters. It is interesting what the Spirit may bring!

This letter is getting long, but here's more about our discussions on the liturgy. A number of bishops spoke about sermons at Mass but the word several used was a new one, "homilies." Our homilies at Mass should be more oriented toward the Holy Scriptures, they said. Recall that at home we priests often followed an outline of scheduled sermons on the sacraments, the commandments, etc., sent to us by the chancery office. What the bishops are suggesting is that scriptural "homilies" would be more complimentary to the wording of the Mass, make the Mass better understood and lived by all of us. Really, when you come to think of it, the first part of the Mass is the teaching portion, which should be connected with the eucharistic sacrifice.

One bishop urged that "Catholics should be better educated regarding the observance of the holy days of obligation." That's been a problem for us bishops in the United States. Not the teaching part but the fact that fewer people come to Church on holy days than on Sundays. I was chairman of our bishops' committee to study holy days in the United States. A study that asked if, because of our lifestyle in the United States, some of the holy days ought to be eliminated or at least transferred to Sunday. Our study revealed that most clergy and religious were in favor of changes but that the laity was not.

November 2, 1962

We're in the midst of a mini-holiday. What with the feast of All Saints and All Souls, the Council sessions were adjourned for five days. One of our parishioners wrote to me and asked: "Bishop, do you have to work all the time in Rome? Do you have any days off?" Perhaps my letters have given the impression that we're pretty busy. Yes, we are working hard, but as I indicated in the beginning of this letter there have been these five days, really an extended weekend of days off.

And as usual I had a chance to do some more wandering around Rome. This time a long walk again down that hill from Via Sardegna to the Piazza di Spagna, a square at the foot of the famous Spanish Steps. At the top of those steps, perhaps a hundred or more of them, is the famous chapel, Trinita dei Monte, which belongs to a religious order of women, containing some rare paintings, even one by Raphael.

At the base of those steps is a forty or fifty-foot column with a statue of the Blessed Virgin at the top. In the four corners at the base that supports the statue are huge figures of the four evangelists. We have an exact replica of that column and its figures at the base of the steps that lead to the main Chapel at our Seminary in Mundelein. I was delighted to see the original.

The other evening we had quite a party. Cardinal Meyer celebrated his feast day and the anniversary of his being named a Cardinal. We went to his titular Church of St. Cecilia in the Transtevere section of Rome, a quaint, very poor yet very interesting area. St. Cecilia's is a very ancient church and stands on the sight of that saint's house. In 821 her body was moved from the Catacombs to a place

Chicago Auxiliary Bishops Aloysius Wycislo, at left, and Cletus O'Donnell are pictured with His Eminence Albert Cardinal Meyer, Archbishop of Chicago during the opening days of Vatican Council II.

beneath the altar of the church while in another part of the church there is a gorgeous recumbent marble statue of St. Cecelia showing her as she was found when her casket was opened in 1599.

At Mass, Bishop O'Donnell and I assisted the Cardinal with some difficulty. The lighting system in the tiny church was very poor and at one point the lights went out entirely. We finished Mass by candlelight. Sounds romantic but to be factual, the church was damp, our hands were cold, and we tripped on the frayed carpeting in the sanctuary.

The dinner that followed in a dungeon-like restaurant called Da Mia Pattaca just around the corner from St. Cecilia's was superb. There the candlelight and rough-hewn tables and benches we sat on were in keeping with the atmosphere of the place. And what a surprise. Msgr. Marcinkus had somehow or other inveigled the director of the Sistine Choir to bring his boys over to entertain us. They sang popular Italian songs that had us humming and foot tapping with them. Later, I went over to the tables where the boys were enjoying their dinner to thank them for the concert. I watched them a while manipulating the antipasto with a table spoon and fork so deftly that I was envious and determined to learn the technique.

But all was not play that weekend. On another evening we joined the other bishops from the United States for several hours at the American College for discussion of our position relative to the changes in the liturgy. We selected several spokesmen who would present our views at St. Peter's during the next sessions of the Council.

Today is Sunday and I write following an interesting afternoon. A bright Italian sun was shining, so instead of the usual post-luncheon nap, I decided on a walk. I made my way through that park I mentioned before, the Villa Borghese, on toward St. Peter's. I stopped to rest at one of those sidewalk cafes, something like a "deli" back home for a cup of "cappuccino."

At another table, a yard or two away from mine, sat a bearded bishop I soon learned was from the missions in New Guinea. Sipping our "cappuccino," we began to talk about the document on the liturgy that was taking up so much of our time at the Council.

Rome offers a strange paradox. It can be the most unworldly city in the world, yet it is the one city that can claim to be central and contemporary with human society. No city in the world, and I've been in many of them, approaches Rome in the interest it elicits from the most widely divergent nations or cultures. Do you wonder then why a young bishop from America can sit down for coffee with another bishop from the other side of the world?

Since neither of us sitting there at a table on the Via Conciliazione were prophets we could not answer the first question that came to our minds when the word liturgy came up. What will this document on the liturgy, especially the use of the vernacular, and so many of the other changes do to us as priests and to those for whom we preside at the Eucharist and at the other sacraments?

We never reached a conclusion but my bearded acquaintance and I parted wishing each other well. But all the way back up the hill to my temporary home in Rome those unanswered questions bothered me. A press release from our Conference offices in Rome provided some light. It quoted Pope John who said:

> "All those arduous and complex debates about the liturgy have not been without fruit. If, at this juncture, we have set out to simplify the external expressions of worship, in an effort to make it more comprehensible to our people and closer to current speech, this does not mean that we wish to reduce the importance of prayer, or put it on a lower plane than other obligations of the sacred ministry or of the apostolate. Neither does it mean that we want to make worship less expressive or less esthetically satisfying. It is rather that we want to make it purer, more genuine, closer to the sources of truth and grace, better fitted to be the spiritual patrimony of the people."

There is just this problem. Suppose I go to China again. I don't speak Chinese. Then what? One bishop at our meeting a week or so ago said: "Why not an ecumenical or world Mass to which we could invite our Protestant friends?" I think he was being facetious. Another bishop suggested that the priest should face the people when celebrating Mass as our Lord did at the Last Supper and, as He did, speak in the language of those present.

My first experience with the vernacular at Mass was not in English but in Italian. I was visiting one of those shrines that dot Rome where apparently some experimentation was being done with the vernacular. The priest was facing the people during that Mass. It was a wonderful experience, that interchange of people and priest praying together.

But there's more. The rite of Baptism is to be shortened – less wear and tear on the baby, but that was not the reason. The rite has been so added to over the years that a simplification is indicated. It was suggested that the Confirmation formulas should be altered; a new form or wording for the sacrament of Penance and many other changes are in the offing if that document on the liturgy goes through. Personally, I hope it does.

November 7, 1962

We're back at work after that brief holiday following the feast day of All Saints. Sunny Italy, is not. Rome is rainy and wet and most every bishop has the sniffles. Maybe the weather has something to do with the present spirit of the Council. There is a bit of impatience in the air. That document on the liturgy has taken up most of our attention for the last month. The Americans are anxious to get things going. We're not used to working, just a half a day, and what with those days off we feel more could be done to move the agenda along. But, most of us are resigned to the life-style here that is expressed in the phrase: "When in

27

Rome, do as the Romans do."

What was unusual about this meeting was the celebration of Mass this morning. The language was in the ancient Syriac, the last stage in the evolution of the Aramaic language spoken by our Lord. The press release from our Conference office advised us that this was the first time that the language Jesus used was heard in St. Peter's Basilica.

Archbishop Felici, the Council's secretary, again reminded those bishops who asked for the floor to be brief and not repeat what was said by another bishop. So it was that among innovations suggested for the liturgy was to reduce or eliminate those prayers we priests say at the foot of the altar as Mass begins.

In our liturgy commission meetings it was suggested that in place of those prayers at the foot of the altar there ought to be an entrance song in which both priests and people participate. And, speaking of participation, discussion centered around the fact that for so long the clergy dominated the sacred functions of the Mass and that the people were simply present as silent spectators, often passive ones at that. If I might sum up a great deal of that philosophy many of us here feel that the liturgy ought to be less clerical, and in a language that people understand. The Mass ought not to be a private function of the priest since the liturgical services pertain "to the whole Body of the Church," as one bishop put it. I was reminded that back in 1956, long before the Council came up with the idea, the Holy Week rites in our parishes were changed to include more participation by the people.

Naturally, there were bishops who feared that the change in the use of Latin language at Mass would disturb those who are attached to the traditional ways of doing things. On the other hand, there were others who felt, as I do, that the reform of the liturgy must harmonize with the way we feel and express ourselves these days. In our country, our religion must reach out into the market-place, otherwise the world in which we live will pass religion by. I think Pope John said something like that in his opening speech to us last October.

In celebrating Confirmations back home, I notice that the spiritual level of a parish can be measured by the quality of its liturgical celebrations. I've noticed here that the missionary bishops particularly are interested in adapting the Mass and the sacraments to their culture. So it's a very bold direction in which we're moving here in this matter of liturgical reform. The test will come when we vote on whether or not to throw off the iron collar of Western and Latin culture that has dominated Catholicism throughout the world.

Well, we've been on this document on the liturgy for almost a month now but I feel that our discussions are beginning to gel. There's been a humorous side to all this too. The other day one of the bishops complained that speeches were too long and too numerous and asked when we were going to begin voting on all those amendments we made. His remarks were greeted with applause.

The Secretary of the Council, Archbishop Felici, begged the bishops that they not repeat what has already been said, that they be brief as possible when they speak. And today, the Presidency of the Council, they're the ten Cardinals that take turns in presiding over the Council, decided to ask us: "Are you agreed that this discussion on the second chapter of liturgy document should end?" A favorable vote was to be expressed by standing, and almost every one of us stood up.

At the end of our thirteenth meeting, the Pope announced that this session of the Council would come to a close on December 8th with a solemn Mass in St. Peter's Basilica. Also, there was talk that the next session would open in May of next year. The Pope however, squelched that rumor by announcing that we would meet again in Rome in September, 1963.

November 13, 1962

I'm sure you recall from a previous letter my reference to that sea of azaleas that flood the Spanish Steps as they climb up the Church of Trinita dei Monte. In any case, this morning, as I reached the top of the long steps up to St. Peter's Basilica for our eighteenth meeting of the Council, I looked back over the Square at a cascade of color that reminded me of those azaleas – the hundreds of bishops in their choir robes. Cardinals in scarlet, archbishops and bishops in magenta and monsignors in their purple cassocks. There they were, the teaching arm of the Church, nodding and talking, swaying and moving in the clear light of a new day.

Bishops tall and thin, some portly, of every size and degree of status. Anyone who has the least sense of history could not but be moved by this meeting of bishops from all over the world, from every nation, each professing a common faith, stemming from a common tradition, on this occasion speaking a common tongue. Here I sensed the profound meaning of the continuity of our faith; here I sensed stability in a world of change.

A strange peace came over me as I took my place among my neighbor bishops to begin another day of Vatican Council II. The world out there was waiting for us, the leaders of the Church, to provide light and direction for that changing world. I think our prayer to the Holy Spirit that morning, at least for me, took on a deeper fervor.

It's been known that the Holy Father has been following the events of our meetings over closed TV. He must have sensed the impatience of the past weeks because he instructed the secretary, Archbishop Felici, to solicit a vote on whether the bishops wanted to continue discussion of the document and/or instruct the Commission on the Liturgy to come up with a final draft. And that we did, 2,209 of us voted to send our deliberations to that special liturgy commission with the request that they provide us with a final text at the next session of the Council.

The Secretary also announced that the next topic following the liturgy will be a discussion of Scripture and Tradition, or what the experts call the two sources of God's revelation to humankind.

There were, however, some left-over liturgical matters that were brought to our attention before we plunged into discussion of the document on revelation.

Cardinal Meyer's intervention on the Breviary provoked other bishops to express themselves about the priest's daily prayer. Some speakers felt that Latin should be retained in the Breviary, others that the size or arrangement of prayers should be reduced to give priests more time for the work of serving the faithful people of God. Others asked that the Breviary be adapted to the time demands and conditions of today's priests.

Other topics relating to liturgy or the sacraments included discussion of the sacrament of Penance, the observance of Sunday Mass, sacred music and art. Regarding Penance, the opinion was expressed that the "traditional forms of penance should be adapted to the requirements of modern life and to the conditions of particular regions, making use of forms which would seem to correspond better to the needs of souls." Under the title of art there was discussion about the proliferation of statues in some of our churches. One of our American bishops known for his humor stated at our coffee break that Europeans who have their churches built by the state don't realize why we memorialize statues in our churches in order to pay off building debts.

A final note. Pope John asked that the name of St. Joseph, foster father of Jesus, be included in the Canon of the Mass. There was some discussion of this, principally about just where St. Joseph would fit in with that list of saints already mentioned in the Mass.

And so ended our long and arduous work on the liturgy that spanned eighteen meetings.

November 21, 1962

The promised document, here we call it a "schema," on Divine Revelation was given us for study almost a week ago just as we were finishing the discussions on liturgy.

Here, at our temporary home in Rome, Cardinal Meyer, who has been on the Preparatory commission considering that schema told us that we would be in for some heated debate because the schema proposes to close the doors on a lot of progress that has been made in the way theologians interpret the scriptures. The very title, "The Sources of Divine Revelation," has been the subject of debate among scripture scholars and theologians for almost four hundred years, ever since the Council of Trent which ended in 1563.

At the heart of the debate has been the phrase, "the two sources of revelation," that came into use among our Catholic scholars in the post-Tridentine period when they were defending one of those sources, Tradition, or the spoken word, against the attacks of Protestant scholars who put all their faith in the Bible only, or the written word.

From Wednesday on through Saturday of last week, as the Cardinal predicted, the fire-works began. Some bishops were so displeased with the schema presented us that they felt it should be entirely rewritten; others suggested that the subject be dropped or at least shelved for the time being. The two experts on the scripture (Fathers Frank McCool and Barnabas Mary Ahearn of the Biblical College in Rome) who were working with our Cardinal, hinted at dinner the other evening that behind the scenes on this matter of Divine Revelation were the same ultra-conservative people who were against the Pope for calling the Council and who were in the vanguard of those opposing the scholars who were teaching the new methods of interpreting the Bible or what I learned later was called a "new biblical theology."

I surmised that these were the self-same curial officials

Bishop Wycislo with the Polish Bishop of Czestochowa at the Second Vatican Council. Bishops were seated at desks in sections according to their year of consecration.

who disagreed with Pope Pius XII in 1943 when he wrote a magnificent encyclical promoting biblical studies which he called, "Divino Afflante Spiritu," in an attempt to calm the troubled waters of scriptural interpretation. That encyclical proposed a whole new scientific approach to biblical studies that encourages scripture scholars. Some of those scholars are here with us as "periti," but it appears that the "hard-heads" among the bishops are at them again.

Last Thursday, November 15 will go down in history. It was the day the famous and almost blind Cardinal Ottaviani, the head of the Holy Office (the "watchdog" agency in the Vatican that controls what is or is not to be taught by the Church) and the head of the Theology Commission responsible for the schema on revelation, introduced that subject with a phrase that he became famous for: "Semper idem," always the same, or as he put it that day: "The truth is everywhere and always the same."

Then the formal interventions began. Cardinal Lienert from France fired the first gun with a phrase that was to be heard again and again, "Mihi non placet," or "it does not please me." Cardinal Ritter of St. Louis went one further and fired both barrels by simply getting up and saying: "Rejiciendum est," or, "throw it out." More politely though, "It must be rejected."

What is at the heart of the debate here is language. Are there one or two ways in which God has revealed his word to us; in writing, by the inspired authors of the Bible, or, by spoken word, or the traditional way in which the faith was practiced? The document we received for discussion speaks of two distinct sources of God's Revelation. It brings up the old argument that the Church has had with Protestants over the centuries about how the Bible is to be understood and interpreted. On the other side are those who ask: "Why bring up the idea of two sources when the Council of Trent, four hundred years ago, affirmed that the written scriptures were the only source of revelation, but that revelation was communicated to us in a twofold manner through scripture and tradition?" Sounds complicated, and it is.

That same evening Cardinal Meyer tipped us off to the news that the members of his Biblical Commission were so concerned with the virulency of the opposition that was being generated that they were prepared to suggest that the Holy Father postpone discussion of the schema on Divine Revelation to the next session of the Council.

In the coffee bars one heard expressions like: "That schema on revelation ought to be scrapped or be entirely redone." "The schema lacks a pastoral tone – it inspires a fear of the scriptures rather than being an inspiration." In any case, the question of further discussion of the scripture document was put in peculiar fashion – a "yes" vote would mean the end of any document on revelation; a "no" vote would indicate that the schema is full of errors, something that would not be true. So great was the confusion about this proposal that the question was presented to us in five languages and several times in Latin. Despite that, the vote lacked the necessary two-thirds majority for passage.

This evening as I write this letter I can report that the Holy Father is stepping into the fray in an effort to settle the matter. Cardinal Cicognani, the Papal Secretary of State, who, by the way, was the Apostolic Delegate to the United States prior to the Council, advised us that according to the wishes of the Holy Father, a special commission would be set up to re-write the proposal in a more acceptable form and guide the bishops through a less intricate document. In the Holy Father's words, "making it shorter and relating it to some of the principles handled by the two previous Councils, Trent and Vatican I.

So you see, there's been a human side to all of our work here. And, speaking of the human side, I should tell you that we get up pretty early here. Mass with the Cardinal in our private Chapel at this House of Studies, breakfast, and by nine we're due at St. Peter's. There, we celebrate another Mass, often in another rite and language just to make us aware of the fact that our Church is not all Western and Latin. Then comes the Enthronement of the Scriptures in which a bishop, flanked by two candle bearers, proceeds down the center aisle of the Basilica to a special table where the sacred Word of God is placed.

Then, maybe an hour or so later, the Secretary makes a number of announcements, some about the work that lies ahead of us, a feast day or a holiday that may interrupt our meetings, the list of those who will speak that day (maybe twenty or thirty names) and the usual admonition that we speak in Latin and within the time allotted.

About eleven o'clock there is an exodus to the coffee bars where one can get a substitute for a breakfast one may have missed. There's the usual very strong demitasse of the Italian version of coffee called "espresso," or the milder "cappuccino," sweet rolls and the like. But you don't have to miss the discussions that are going on inside the Basilica; loudspeakers keep us informed of what's going on and repeatedly advise us if a vote is imminent.

The Council Presidency selects one of its members to lead our debates, or more politely, direct the numerous interventions that make up the morning. Now and then an animated bishop gets up, or there is a sensational new proposal, and some 2,000 pairs of eyes are focused on one man's voice. One morning a bishop speaking Latin with a Spanish accent, making understanding difficult, was gesticulating and speaking so loudly into the microphone that my neighbor from Canada remarked: "Listen to him, preaching to preachers."

Before our meeting ended today, the Secretary announced that while the special commission was working on the Scripture document, we would get into the next item on the agenda that has to do with communications.

Generally our meetings end by one o'clock. Bishop O'Donnell and I head for the back door of St. Peter's where we will meet the Cardinal and Msgr. Bergin, our chauffeur. Back at the House of Studies there's lunch and the inevitable bottle of wine that probably accounts for that need of a nap I'm getting accustomed to.

I had not done any homework on that communications document the Secretary announced, so I asked the Cardinal about it. He had heard that we would be presented with a document spelling out the importance of communications as a means of spreading the Gospel and the use of the media as a teaching arm of the Church.

November 26, 1962

Last Thursday, Friday and Saturday – oh yes, we work on Saturdays – that proposal on the use of the modern means of communications came up. Not much has been or will be accomplished in that area apparently because only this morning, our twenty-seventh meeting, we were told that discussion on communications would end and we would move on to discussions about reconciliation with our separated brethren of the Eastern Churches.

It seems that the initial thrust of the paper they gave us on communications is based on the obligation of the Church, on an international, national and diocesan level, to informing and forming public opinion on matters of social justice, the dignity of the human person, etc. We were also told that proposals before us on the communications media were drawn up by Archbishop Martin O'Connor, an American, and the head of our American College in Rome.

The communications document, a short one, was explained to us by several members of that Communication commission. Judging from the reactions to what was said by those members, there surfaced a favorable feeling for the proposals. One heard phrases like: "The media are a source of entertainment for the modern world." "Communications should never be indifferent to the moral force they exert . . . especially among the young who make up the majority of the audience." "The Church needs to learn how to use the media for the preaching of the Gospel to see to it that the media not be allowed to destroy the moral or religious aspects of society." I wonder if the media people will be listening.

This morning discussion on the subject of communications came to an end with the promise that we would be taking up the subject again at a later date.

We moved into that matter of those separated Eastern churches, a subject that is part of the ecumenical movement which aims at the eventual reunion of all the Christian Churches, something which Pope John had in mind when he called his bishops to Rome for a Council. The discussion will, of course, be of great personal interest to me. During the years of the Second World War, while I was engaged in the relief and rehabilitation programs for the victims of that war on behalf of the American bishop's Catholic Relief Services, I was closely involved in conversations with other Christian and with Jewish organizations in common efforts to heal the wounds of war. That is probably why the President of our National Conference of Bishops asked me to serve on the commission for Ecumenical Affairs here in Rome.

You are probably not aware of this, but that suggestion to begin reunion with our Eastern Christians centers around a long history of relationships wherein there is a unity in faith, but disagreement on some teachings of the Church, such as unity with the Pope.

The press bulletin we received at the end of the day stated: "The document the bishops would receive discusses the theological unity of the Church which is based on the unity of government, that is, upon Peter and his successors. Account was taken of the difficulties which separated Oriental brothers have in accepting this truth."

One bishop put the whole problem in a nutshell when he said: "We should distinguish between what separates Catholics from Eastern Christians and what separates Catholics and Protestants. The elements which unite us are greater than those which separate us." I feel that future discussions on ecumenism ought to be directed to the positive – that which unites us – rather than the negative, that which divides.

I'll have to write more on this subject as we move along in these final weeks of the Council's first session. So many things are piling up on my desk here. There are two or three other schemata that will be coming up before heading for home. Something about a document on the nature of the Church; about the powers of bishops and the relationship of bishops to the Pope; some final decisions to be made about the liturgy text that we hope might be approved in this session. Some bishops are pushing for a discussion on the doctrine of the Mystical Body of Christ. Oh yes, and there is talk about more of the laity should be involved as experts to advise the bishops. Presently, most of the periti or experts are priests.

December 7, 1962

Excitement abounds. Tomorrow will be the last meeting of this session of Vatican II. There seems to be a rush to get ever so many things done. We're being flooded with papers and it will take the next nine months to digest the material at home in preparation for the next session of the Council.

And we had a surprise visit from the Pope today. All of a sudden, about halfway through the morning, the Secretary interrupted our discussion to tell us that the Pope had decided to visit us for a while. The Holy Father was greeted with applause. We had been hearing rumors that he was not feeling well. He raised our spirits right away when he said: "I've been closer to you than you think, close to you in prayer and close to you in thought because our pastoral mission has as its sole objective the spreading of the Gospel and its penetration of our times. I look forward to tomorrow's ceremony when we officially end this session of the of the Council and I pray for your safe return home."

Last Thursday, the Secretary shared some interesting information with us. During the thirty-four meetings, 587 bishops had spoken from the floor of St. Peter's and 523 had made available their interventions in writing. We were also reminded that some weeks ago we had received the preliminary draft of the document on the nature of the Church and that we would begin discussion of that material before this session of the Council ended.

So it was that last Saturday we began discussion of the schema on the Church. An interesting document it is, at least from my quick scanning of the eighty-page text. One bishop called it the "master document of the Council." It treats of matters like who are the People of God, the hierarchy or bishops, the laity, religious, what are our obligations as members of the Church, etc. There was a brief skirmish when several bishops urged discussion of a shorter five-page paper on the Blessed Virgin Mary in place of the schema on the Church, reasoning that the latter was so long that we would not have time to do it justice. We were told that since the presenter of that Marian document, Cardinal Ottaviani, had not followed channels in presenting the proposal we would broach the schema on the Church instead.

I should mention that as we approached the beginning of the Council last October there were some seventy documents that the Preparatory commissions had listed as a result of the inquiries Pope John made of us bishops. Now, because of the many requests for a more streamlined agenda, we're down to twenty schemas, and that number may even be reduced in the next few months. We were told that when the special coordinating committee the Pope appointed to revise the number and content of those twenty documents had finished its work, we would be mailed a new listing along with some completed documents for our study.

While we plunged into the schema on the Church we also proceeded with voting on the amendments to the liturgy document. We had high hopes that the liturgy document would be the first schema to be published as a result of the first session of the Council. That was not to be. Time ran out. We were able to vote approval only on the preface and the first chapter. But that was just as well. The preface contained the general principles for liturgical reform in which many of us were interested. Some of those principles included the introduction of the vernacular languages in various parts of the Mass, the adoption of certain local customs in the way Mass is to be celebrated, and, above all, the very active participation of the people in the Mass. I have a note on the margin of the liturgy document that states 1,922 bishops voted in favor of the preface and first chapter; 11 against and there were 180 "maybe" votes.

Decisions about celebrating the new liturgies including all the sacraments would be handled by our Bishops' Conference in Washington in consultation with Rome. The funeral rites will be changed; white vestments instead of black in keeping with the thought that death is a resurrection to new life; marriage and baptismal ceremonies will be different, etc.

As is evident from this letter, we did not get much done on the Church document. Again and again, one or another bishop spoke, between those liturgy votes, about how important would be that schema on the Church and that it may well turn out to be the most important work of this Council. More to come.

As we bishops close these long, hard weeks of study and decision, there seems to submerge for me a patter, perhaps a theme which dominated the planning and discussions of this first session of Vatican II, namely, what is this Church of ours in this modern world? How will she answer the needs and desires of her children all over the world, and how effective will she be in showing each of us the way to save our souls? Those exhaustive years of travel I did during the Second World War years on behalf of the suffering, homeless, and sick exposed me to a world looking for peace and the presence of God in our world affair.

These meetings in St. Peter's where I mingled and listened to bishops from every part of the world gave me new perspective. The Church needs to penetrate the world, provide new and attractive means to heal it. The entire Church will have to learn to adapt to the different cultures that have absorbed the faith but are not always at home with it. The so-called national churches want to be heard and listened to. I have a feeling that the next session of the Council will recognize and address that concern.

A second impression I have is that the Church, as I perceive its presence here in the persons of the bishops who lead it, wants very much to develop those movements that are so spontaneously surging and pulsating in the Mystical Body of Christ. I feel the awakening of a whole Church in its liturgical, biblical and catechetical life. I sense a new role for the laity in the Church.

One bishop said to me, as we were walking out of St. Peter's: "I hope we don't rock St. Peter's boat too badly when we return next year."

December 9, 1962

Tomorrow we'll be leaving for home. I'm all packed and it's Sunday with a whole afternoon free. I walked that familiar hill down from the Villa Bourghese through the streets that lead to St. Peter's Basilica. I stopped again for a "cappuccino" and went on into the square in front of St. Peter's. I looked up toward the Holy Father's apartment but the shutters were drawn; he had opened them earlier for the noontime Angelus. I guess I just wanted to say my own goodbye to the Pope.

For quite a while I just stood there in that square listening to the two fountains and looking up at the obelisk that dominates it. Then I heard the chimes from the gate of the bells that marked the hour, it was three in the afternoon. I circled the colonnades that surround the square and looked up at the coigns at the top – those baroque sculptures for bygone saints, and of SS. Peter and Paul, who dominate the entrance to the basilica. I wondered what they thought of us bishops who came to work at revitalizing the faith, much in the same way that they worked at it in the first Council in Jerusalem.

I walked into the dark interior of Christendom's greatest Church, to Peter's tomb surrounded by a hundred vigil lights, knelt and prayed: "Lord, pour forth your grace into our hearts. Grant us a safe journey home to those you have asked us to serve. Help us to share in truth what Peter's successor has asked us to do."

Between First Session and Second Session

December 16, 1962 - September 29, 1963

December 16, 1962

Now that I am home, I can tell you about our last working day in Rome. On December 8th, there was the solemn closing of the first session of Vatican II in the great Basilica of St. Peter's. But first this bit of news. Cardinal Meyer, somewhere over the North Atlantic, turned to me and said: "Bishop, I'd like to you to organize and chair a liturgical commission in our archdiocese for implementing that document on the liturgy. True, it's not completed, but there will be much to be done and it will give your commission members an incentive to study the progress of the schema on the liturgy when we return to Rome next year."

The Pope was not present at the Mass of the Immaculate Conception. Cardinal Marcella, who is a kind of "major domo" for the Basilica of St. Peter's, celebrated the Mass. Rumor had it that the Pope was seeing his doctor, who apparently allowed the ailing Holy Father to visit and say goodbye to us after all. So it was that as soon as the Mass was over, the Pope appeared at the front doors of the Basilica. He was greeted with tremendous applause and proceeded to walk the length of St. Peter's to a special throne in front of the main altar while the choir sang the very moving hymn "Tu es Petrus," "Thou art Peter."

A bit drawn in face, the Holy Father addressed us for about thirty minutes. He reminded us that the day's celebration does not bring our work to an end. He hinted that we would have much to do before we returned to Rome next September. Aware of our disagreements, he said: "The sometimes sharply divergent views of the Council Fathers manifested during the first session were a healthy demonstration to the world of the holy liberty that exists within the Church."

"It was no accident," said the Pope, that the "liturgy document was the first to be considered by the Council. After all, the liturgy defines the relationship between us and God. It is the highest form of relationship and is based on the solid foundation of Revelation and apostolic teaching."

And then the Pope reminded us again that although we would be busy with our diocesan tasks when we get home, he hoped that "we would continue to investigate and study the schemas that had been provided us and those that would be mailed to us in the future."

His parting words stirred every one of our hearts:

"Godspeed to you, we will meet here again," and quoting a phrase of Pope Pius IX at the first Vatican Council, he ended with his blessing and these words: "Peace, as you know, casts our fear; peace shuts its ears to what is said without real knowledge. May this peace be yours all the days of your life."

And so ended that first meeting of the world's bishops whom Pope John called to Rome to "study the signs of the times." Later that day I took another walk about Rome. This time to audit the Press Panel on the Council held forth on the Via Conciliazione. The reporters were anxious to get the reactions of the American bishops to the first session of the Council. Most were inquisitive about the Pope's health and information on that subject was understandably meager.

Archbishop Hallinan of Atlanta gave a very positive picture of the future of liturgy in the Church. That controversial document on Revelation, explained one of the bishops,

45

would return to us before the next session with lesser input from the conservatives in the Vatican offices who were, from the very beginning, against any consideration of the double sources of Revelation.

And speaking of conservatives, our friend, the expert who assisted our Cardinal Meyer, Father Francis McCool, in answering a reporter's question about how you tell a conservative from a progressive made this sage remark: "A progressive looks to the future and sees promise in it; a conservative looks to the future and see a threat to the past."

I think a lot of us bishops went to Rome as conservatives and learned that the inertia in the Church that Pope John was trying to challenge turned a good number of us into progressives. After all, we were products of the old school, given that our average age was in the late fifties.

Another tid-bit: I learned at that press conference that Pope John appointed two Cardinals to share the presidency of that all-important special commission to recast the document on Revelation: Cardinal Bea, a renowned biblical scholar and a "progressive," and Cardinal Ottaviani, a great theologian with firm conservative leanings. Bea is the head of the Secretariat for Promoting Christian Unity and Ottaviani is the head of the Theology Commission in the Council. I mentioned earlier that Cardinal Meyer was a member of that special commission and now would be making occasional trips to Rome to meet with that group.

I brought back with me a copy of the official Vatican newspaper, *L'Osservatore Romano*. Little did I realize how important that copy would be for me given the Cardinal's request that I organize and head a Liturgical Commission for the Archdiocese of Chicago. The paper contained an extensive commentary by a Father Vagaggini, a liturgical scholar who was one of the experts brought to Rome by the Pope.

A few lines from the commentary: "The use of the Latin

language is to be preserved in the Mass . . . but since the use of the vernacular in the Mass, the sacraments and other liturgical rites, can be very helpful to the people, a larger role should be given to the languages of the various peoples." Another, and what I feel will be a welcome change, the liturgy should be "adapted to the customs of various races and peoples." A cautionary sentence added to that privilege emphasizes that such adaptation should not be bound up with superstition and error." I forsee some problems here with those who are against change or who are inclined to superstition.

Now that I'm back home with you, my weekly articles in our parish bulletin will now and then continue with those letters from Rome. There is more about the liturgy I would like to share with you and no doubt you will be interested in what we bishops are about between sessions of the Council. In other words, I'll share with you whatever I can of the homework that has been assigned to us.

January 8, 1963

Would it not have been great if we could have celebrated our Christmas and New Year Masses in the vernacular – that great highlight of the document on the Sacred Liturgy that has come out of our first session of Vatican II. I'll have more to tell you about the future of our liturgy as the months go by. As of now, it's good to be home but the experience of those months in Rome still has me agog. It's been difficult to adjust to the routine concerns of our parish but our ever-efficient parish assistants are helping me.

As we move into the year ahead, I'll try to keep you abreast now and then of the preparations we are making for the next session of Vatican II. There will, of course, be the scheduled meetings of the various commissions in Rome which some of our American bishops will have to attend. I know the Cardinal expects to be making a few trips.

I will be active also in those commissions that will be meeting in Washington on matters that pertain to the Council work to which I have been appointed. As I get the reports I'll try to share what I can with you. Understandably some things will have to be kept secret so as to not create misunderstanding. Fragmentary information can do more harm than good.

As I look back over the first session of the Council, several things stand out. There was a start in eliminating the incompatibility between the documents that were given us in Rome on our arrival and the desires of most of the bishops who sincerely grasped Pope John's desire for renewal. I would suspect that when we return from the next session that desire will be deepened. I did mention to you that there were a total of some seventy schemas presented, but these will necessarily be whittled down as the commissions begin work on them. Again, I suspect that there will be more groupings of subject matter and even more effort to shorten some of the documentation. The schema on the Nature of Church is quite a volume as is the one on Divine Revelation.

One improvement that took hold a little late in the first session was the relationship between the media people and those who were dispensing information about what was happening inside St. Peter's. The Council sessions were to be kept secret and we were cautioned to be circumspect about what we said outside the Council meetings. One of the reasons I wrote those letters to you was to correct the sometimes misleading information you might have been getting from the press and television. It was not their fault entirely; they had to do a lot of "snooping" to get information. To correct that situation and to put things in proper perspective, the American bishops set up a Press Panel every afternoon. I have heard that plans are in the making to improve the methods of dispensing information about our future Council sessions.

February 5, 1963

Very soon I'll be getting involved in that new work the Cardinal has assigned to me, the organizing of a Liturgical Commission for the Archdiocese of Chicago. His Eminence has given me access to his library and the collection of literature he has accumulated over the years on the subject. I was particularly intrigued with a professional magazine he had subscribed to over the years called *Worship*. It comes out of St. John's University in Collegeville, Minnesota.

Poring over those old magazines and seeking out whatever books I could find on the subject of liturgy, I soon learned that our first session of Vatican II on the liturgy was not innovative. Changes in the worship practices of the Church had been going on for at least fifty years prior to the Council. Names like Virgil Michael who produced the first issue of *Worship* twenty-five years ago; Godfrey Diekman of Collegeville, Minnesota, Prosper Gueranger, Louis Bouyer of France, Josef Jungmann of Germany, Martin Hellriegal, Frederick McManus of the United States and others were pioneers in the movement for change.

I really believe that it was Pope Pius XII's 1947 encyclical on the liturgy, "Mediator Dei," that became the Magna Carta of the liturgical movement. It opened our eyes to change during those early sessions of the Council last year. Prior to the Council, our liturgy was fixed, rubrical dominated by the clergy. What the future holds is a liturgy that will allow for variety, option and flexibility. It will seriously encourage the participation and the involvement of the worshipping community.

Then too, you must remember the changes in the liturgy that became part of parish life in the ten or so years prior to the Second Vatican Council. Pope Pius XII introduced changes in the Holy Week liturgies, e.g.; people began to use the Latin – English Missal at Mass, a forerunner of the greater participation in the Mass that our first session at Vatican II was promoting. Some of the younger generation will recall the Missa Luba in which the meeting of two cultures took place – African and European. It was an attempt to harmonize our Roman liturgy with the wealth and beauty of Congolese music. And there were the beat of the drums with that too, remember?

Do you remember the introduction of evening Masses in the 1950's and the reduction and practical abolition of the Eucharistic fast? In 1939, Pope Pius XII recognized the legitimacy of Chinese rites. And so much preceded what some thought were the radical changes in liturgy initiated by Vatican II.

Fifteen general meetings of the Council were devoted to the liturgy schema. It was the only document not rejected or returned for complete revision. That reflected not only the nature of the good preparation that went into the document, but also the vigorous work of the liturgical movements I spoke about earlier. Many of those men whose names I mentioned were in Rome with us as experts and advisors. Thus it was that our first session of Vatican II confirmed the liturgical movement which was supported by a biblical movement and a renewal of catechetics and preaching of the Word together into a coherent whole.

March 19, 1963

As with the liturgical movement that gave initiative to many changes authorized by Vatican II, so in other fields there were movements that antedated the Council and had an influence on our deliberations. Reflection on the liturgy naturally lead to reflection on the Nature of the Church. The bishops are presently studying such a document, a document theologians have been mulling over for years, often to their discredit. Pope John brought many of those theologians as experts to the Council and they'll probably see the fruition of their efforts, as did the men who pushed for the changes in the liturgy.

Another schema we have at hand for serious consideration in the next session of the Council is the document on Revelation, the study and interpretation of the Sacred Scriptures. Here again, as I hinted earlier in my letters, much good work was going on before we got to Rome. Remember how I suggested that Pope Pius XII's encyclical, "Divino Afflante Spiritu" gave encouragement to scripture scholars to pursue their research in the way the Bible was to be interpreted.

Cardinal Meyer told me the other day that he would be flying to Rome for the first of several meetings of the special commission on which he serves to revamp the document on Revelation that caused such a stir in the early part of our first session. Let me review a bit of history for you.

What is Revelation? It's the way God communicated and continues to communicate with us. It's "the how" of this that was at the heart of the difficulties we faced in the first session of the Council when consideration of "the how" came up. The parameters are these – the difinitive revelation of God was communicated to us by Jesus Christ and his apostles. A nice passage from St. Paul's letter to the Ephesians says it this way: "God chose to reveal himself and to make known to us the hidden purpose of his will, by which through Christ, the Word made flesh, a man has access to the Father in the Holy Spirit and comes to share in the divine nature" (Eph.1/9; 2/18).

How is God revealed to us after the apostles died? In two ways, via the scriptures or the written word communicated by the Holy Spirit to the evangelists and by Tradition, or by word of mouth, the way it is preached, or in the way the written word is interpreted by scripture scholars.

Another way of looking at it comes from the fact that the apostles appointed bishops as their successors, as the document we're studying puts it, "handing over their own teaching role" to them. And that same document explains: "This sacred tradition, therefore, and sacred Scripture of both the Old and New Testament are like a mirror in which the pilgrim Church on earth looks at God."

It's a complicated subject, so let me put it another way. Revelation is understood to be a complete, definitive, and unrepeatable self-communication of God through Jesus Christ. At the same time, the official Church also calls Revelation a present reality because of the way God reveals Himself to us through His Son and through the Church. Remember that Christ, just before his Ascension, assured his apostles that, "the Holy Spirit, the Paraclete," would be sent to the Church.

There is something I see coming out of our discussions at the Council on the Liturgy and on Revelation. You will notice in the new style of worship a greater emphasis on the use the scripture writings. It will no longer be a sermon that you will be listening to but a homily, an explanation and application of the readings from the Bible. The priest will be expected to give a homily at every Mass at which there is present a respectable number of people.

So you see, those pre-conciliar movements I wrote to you about, the biblical and liturgical are being fused together. I see a bright future in all that. I see biblical and liturgical renewal playing an important role in the way the Word of

God is used and applied in our public worship of God. I also feel that if you apply Pope John's request to us bishops to "study the signs of the time," there will need to be a sensitivity for what is relevant and contemporary to Christianity in our time.

The document on Revelation is trying to encourage easy access to the Bible, as a book open to all and not just to priests and scholars. The Council is trying to emphasize that the liturgy of the Word and the liturgy of the Sacrament are inseparable. It used to be that when you came to Sunday Mass you could miss the early part, the readings, and still fulfill your obligation.

April 16, 1963

Maybe a little review will be of help to those who are just catching up with "My Letters from Rome." The Second Vatican Council about which I've been writing to you, in the mind of Pope John XXIII who called us bishops to Rome, is to be a council of reform or renewal with a spiritual and pastoral thrust. As the pastor of a large parish in the urban conglomerate of Chicago, I felt that I was in touch with the pastoral needs of the people I was called to serve. I had a feeling about the changes that were necessary to make our Church relevant to our day.

Thus is was that the Holy Father's words last December 7th, the day before the first session of the Council ended, struck home. He said: "Our ministry has no other purpose and desire than that the Gospel of Christ be better known by the men of our time, that it be willingly applied and that it enter always more deeply into all the realms of life."

I really felt the meaning and saw the application of those words of our Holy Father during that first session of meetings in Rome. But I, like other pastoral bishops, sensed the opposition to renewal that came out of some of the leading members of the Pope's very own staff. One got the impression: "Don't rock the boat – the senile old man who called this Council is opening a can of worms."

Enough of that! As I look back over the past months, the spiritual thrust of the Council was indeed pastoral. This was evident not only in the way the Gospel message pervaded all of our discussions, but in the way in which the actual words of that message were written into the documents we were considering. The document on the Liturgy, our first work, is a good example. I see in the other schemas we have before us for study in the next session, the same application of the treasures of the Gospel message.

The reform or renewal of the Church is not a new idea. We have a Latin expression that says: "Ecclesia semper reformanda," meaning "the Church ever to be reformed." Church history reveals periods during which our Church needed to call its members to reform. I recall from my seminary studies how the religious or monastic orders led movements to reform the life-style not only of the Church but also of its members. Did you know that in the Middle Ages it was the Irish monks who introduced the idea of confession, penance and reform into Western Europe?

The word "reform," as I used it has nothing to do with heresy. It is not to be associated with Protestantism despite the fact that I read in some of our Catholic conservative papers that, for instance, some of the changes in the liturgy, are aping Protestant practices. Over the centuries, many of those who brought reforms to the Church were saints.

At the heart of reform or renewal there has always been the notion of conversion (maybe some of the curial officials at the Vatican who oppose the Council, or the conservatives who dislike change, don't like that). We need always to re-direct our lives toward Christ in a world that reeks of sin, infidelities and weaknesses. Holiness is one of the marks of the Church. Don't we, in the Creed, say the Church is One, Holy, Catholic and Apostolic?

Pope John in his opening talk to the Council last October emphasized the need for spiritual renewal, an inner spiritual purification of the Church and its members. He was articulating at a positive form of reform or conversion, a new Pentecost, and said: "It is clear that the grace of the Holy Spirit fills the hearts of the bishops, of the theologians and of all those who are working for this Council."

While emphasizing the spiritual thrust of the Council, Pope John insisted from the very beginning that Vatican II must be essentially a pastoral council, that any theological concepts or new doctrine we bishops came up with had to be pastoral oriented. That kind of pastoral orientation became quite evident in the document on the liturgy we'll be finalizing in the next session. The document and the changes it will effect are directed to the needs of modern life and culture in such a way that our new worship practices can reveal more clearly the presence of Christ in our lives.

Those practices will also open up esteem for the priesthood of the laity by virtue of Baptism and a more active participation in the Mass. In the reading of the scriptures, through preaching and the homily, the awareness of the presence of Christ should become more evident. St. Paul's letter to the Hebrews puts that well: "For the word of God is alive, efficacious and sharper than a two-edged sword."

Another look at reform may take this direction. From the principle of greater lay participation in the liturgical life of the Church broader participation of the laity in the apostolic work of the Church may arise affecting how our bishops and priests administer the Church. We're no longer an immigrant Church in the United States. We have a well educated and spiritually mature laity ready to take their place beside bishop and priest in responsibility for the broader mission of the Church. A document on the Nature of the Church spells out the role of the laity in making the Church more visible.

Another schema, the one on Revelation fosters a better knowledge of the Bible by the laity. It could bring about the end of an individually-centered devotional piety and enhance biblical and liturgical worship practices.

May 14, 1963

Last month, I implied that there was opposition to the calling of an ecumenical council of the Church. Pope John himself made reference to "those prophets of doom," who saw nothing good coming out of a gathering of the bishops of the world. Some of the literature that reached my desk indicates that a conservative element in the Church is organizing against any changes or reform in the Church. Since I was ordained a priest in 1934, I noticed two orientations or movements. One, a progressive openness to change; and the other, a closing in on those who would move the Church into new fields, for example, in liturgy, the more advanced and scientific interpretation of Sacred Scriptures, and toward better relationships with other religions.

After my seminary years I was reading books on "the new theology," books by men like Fathers de Lubac, Danielou, Congar, and an American Jesuit, Father John Courtney Murray. In my travels, especially in France, I ran across "worker priests," men who went into the factories and fields to reach their people; in Africa I witnessed a new culture that was at odds with the Western way of doing things; in South America I witnessed a Church struggling to lift its poor out of the grasp of the ruling and very few rich families that dominated their lives.

Here in our own country, I watched priest friends, like Father Higgins and Cantwell of our own diocese, striving to bring about some understanding with the organized labor unions that were exploiting workers. That leadership became suspect, some even referred to as communists. In 1950 an encyclical came out of Rome, "Humani Generis," that "condemned false opinions threatening to undermine the foundations of Catholic doctrine." Believe it nor not, that encyclical marked with suspicion the men whom I mentioned above. Some were told to stop writing and speaking. It is hard to believe that Pope Pius XII, who wrote that encyclical, had preciously given the Church several other positive and progressive documents.

But, Pope John, even in the face of the opposition he was getting from within his own offices, called many I mentioned earlier to Rome to act as advisors to the bishops at the Council! The Pope apparently saw the need for the Church to move away from its suspicions of the modern world and to open itself up to dialogue. He did not see in Modernism the evil that some thought was there.

Did you know that when I became your pastor I had to take an oath against Modernism? As I became familiar with that movement, there were some positive things about it and some negative aspects. I'm afraid that "the powers that be" in our Church leaned more toward the negative view.

Maybe I've given you the impression that Pope John moved too precipitously into the reason for calling of a Council of the universal Church. I don't think so, because he must have been aware of the great forward steps toward change and renewal that his predecessor Pope Pius XII had taken. By way of example, Pope Pius issued the encyclical on the Mystical Body of Christ "Mystici Corporis" in 1943 which emphasized the sacramental nature of the Church and which is having an impact on our discussions about changes in the Liturgy and worship practices of the Church.

And again in 1943, he gave us the great scriptural document "Divino Afflante Spiritu," which recognized the new scientific methods of interpreting the text of the Bible. That encyclical will continue to have great influence in our discussions of the schema on Divine Revelation which is coming up in the next session of the Council. And another important encyclical, "Mediator Dei," in 1947 influenced our debates on changes in the liturgy.

So you see, Pope John, while breaking new ground, was building on the good works of others.

June 7, 1963

You will remember that soon after the first session of the Council ended I shared with you the news of Pope John's failing health. "My bags are packed," he is reported to have said to one of his aides, and then he went on to say, "and I am ready for the journey." The news stories reaching us from the Vatican last month seemed to indicate that the Pope was in and out of a series of comas. The end for the gentle Pope John came on Monday evening, June 3rd. A courageous heart was stilled. I prayed that this man of peace and love would find the fulfillment of his desires in the embrace of our Lord whom he tried so hard to imitate.

Despite those long months of illness he worked on and left us a legacy that I'm sure will be considered the masterwork of his life, the encyclical, "Pacem in Terris," "Peace on Earth." Here are a few quotes that range from the individual responsibility for peace as well as that of nations:

"Every man is endowed with intelligence and free will. By virtue of this, he has rights and duties of his own, flowing directly and simultaneously from his very nature . . . he has the right to freedom in searching for truth and in expressing and communicating his opinions."

In that passage Pope John was reflecting so much of the freedom of expression that he encouraged during the first session of the Council, and much of that same freedom will be reflected in the future documents of the Council. For instance, in the first document of the Council on the Liturgy, I wonder if a new freedom of expression will bring about abuse and dissent in the unity Pope John prayed for. I wonder too, when we get back to Rome for the next session in the fall, if the opponents to the Council will respect the individual bishop's rights to express himself.

Pope John also said that the duties of individuals are inseparably linked with their rights and that every person has the duty of respecting the rights of others. He emphasized that we must be guided by the principles of truth, justice, charity and freedom.

As far as the wider world, the Pope reminds us and especially temporal authorities, that all "authority derives from God." All men have the right to choose those who will rule the state, to decide the form of government and to determine the limits and the way in which authority is to be exercised.

July 9, 1963

Pope John is dead but the great work on the Second Vatican Council will go on. Pope Paul VI, Archbishop of Milan, Italy and former Secretary of State to Pope Pius XII, was elected on June 21st, to the See of Peter. Unlike Pope John, the new Holy Father is of slight build and has some of the acetic features of Pope Pius XII. Pope John came from a poor farm family in Northern Italy, whereas the new Pope comes of a well-placed background. His roots were planted in the city of Brescia, just 25 miles from Bergamo where Pope John was born. His father was the well-to-do editor of a paper and served several terms in the Italian Parliament. Thus his son, now pope, was exposed very early in his life to Italian politics and diplomacy.

Despite their different roots, both Pope John and Pope Paul had a common interest – their priesthood – the love for people, and a high degree of humility that was permeated with pastoral interest in the good of the Church.

It was my privilege to have worked with the new pope when he was Archbishop Montini in the Secretariat Office of the Vatican. We quickly discovered a common bond. The

Archbishop served in the Apostolic Nuntiature in Poland, thus linking us together by my work with Polish refugees. We collaborated together in planning Vatican relief efforts in the Middle East for thousands of Polish refugees and at the same time for some forty thousand Italians who were interned as prisoners of war near Cairo, Egypt.

Between 1943-1945, the Middle East, Palestine Iran, Iraq, India, Pakistan and a good part of East Africa were deluged with the victims of war who had escaped through what Winston Churchill called the under-belly of Europe.

Soon after his election, Pope Paul VI announced that he would reconvene the Second Vatican Council and paid this tribute to his predecessor:

"At the outset of our pontifical ministry, the memory of those who preceded me comes tenderly and pleasantly to mind. I wish to recall in a special way, with grateful and deeply-moved reverence, the figure of the mourned Pope John XXIII, who in the brief but highly intense span of his ministry knew how to win over to himself the hearts of men, even those who are far away, through his sleepless solicitude, his sincere and concrete kindness toward the lowly and the outstanding pastoral character of his actions, qualities to which were added the very special enchantment of the human gifts of his great heart."

The Pope went on to say in his first public address: "The preeminent part of our Pontificate will be the continuation of the Second Vatican Ecumenical Council, on which are fixed the eyes of all men of good will. This will be the principal task for which we intend to expend all our energies."

In the words of a close friend, Jean Guitton, a French writer, "Pope John had had a vision. That vision has to be changed into reality, into history, and Paul VI was providentially chosen to do just that."

Having therefore, known the two Popes, I too can identify with Jean Guitton's observation. Unlike Pope John XXIII, Pope Paul VI is less open to self-revelation. Pope

John XXIII kept a diary, but I doubt that Paul VI has one. It will be interesting if some day that diary is published. It will reveal more about a man who wanted to walk into your heart.

I remember an audience in which Pope John XXIII was addressing a group of us American bishops. His secretary handed him a prepared text. After getting through the first page the Holy Father simply let the pages fall to the floor, some twenty or so, and said, "Basta," enough of this. Palms up, he raised his hands toward us and said: "I wish to speak to you from the heart." He went on to tell us how he felt and what his dreams were for us and the Council.

"The heart should not have to be separated from the mind," said Jean Guitton. "The charm of Christianity as one sees it in St. Paul, St. John and the Gospels, is to unite mind and heart, thought and love." I often witnessed Pope John XXIII do that. With our new Pope it will be a bit different, he will be on his guard, careful about word and gesture. For him, his intuitive mind will come first, and then he will show heart through those deep penetrating eyes, a slight smile, but never, never, letting slip to the floor the text of formal speech.

Comparisons can be odious. Yet I contrast these two popes for you to show how one complimented the other. The jovial, easy to be with, and extrovert Pope John XXIII, the cerebral, be patient, and cautious Pope Paul VI. The Council will bear the stamp of Pope John XXIII's personality, and its implementation, the careful and studious direction of Pope Paul VI.

August 20, 1963

As I indicated earlier in some of my letters to you, there has been much "homework" in preparation for the next session of the Council which we now know will begin on September 30th. The solemn opening will take place on Sunday, the 29th, and we've already made our travel arrangements.

Part of our homework included several trips to Washington where I serve on the Bishops' Committee on the Liturgy and a meeting here in Chicago of our whole conference of bishops at the Palmer House. I learned much from these meetings and from the information given us by the cardinals, bishops and periti who had attended meetings of the particular commissions on which they serve in Rome.

For instance, the Coordinating Commission, appointed by Pope John XXIII at the end of our first session, had the task of supervising the ten official conciliar commissions. Apparently it has done a marvelous job in bringing down the number of schema from 74 to 16. At hand I have the improved version of the document on the Liturgy, the almost new document on Divine Revelation, and an interesting draft of a document about the Church in the Modern World, a more complete version of the schema on Communications which we debated briefly last fall, a proposal for a document on our relationships with other Christians and with Jews, and, of course, a batch of new regulations, mostly related to the public media, a greater openness because of the importance of the mass media (press, film, radio, and television), and changes in what we will wear during the working sessions of the Council.

There will be before us a most interesting schema on the Church. There was such an interest and favorable reaction to that document in the first session that I look forward to it this time around. I note already from our meetings the enthusiasm for a Constitution on the Church, something about the People of God and the proper dignity and vocation of the layperson. There's a chapter on the role of bishops, on religious, and one on the universal call to holiness on the part of all the People of God.

It appears that we will have a very busy round of meetings come September. Despite all my world travels, I still get that warm feeling about returning to Rome and the opportunities to renew friendships with bishops from so many countries where I worked during the war years.

September 17, 1963

We'll be off for Rome and the meeting of the second session of the Vatican Council within the week. I'm excited about that, not just for the trip and of being in Rome again, but the renewed feeling of hope for the Church. Having gone through the experience of the first session and experiencing a certain bit of anxiety about what an ecumenical council was all about, there's an eagerness to get back to work at that little desk in St. Peter's. Cardinal Meyer has had to make several trips to Rome as a member of the special committee appointed to revise the document on Revelation. The other day he told me that Pope Paul has really taken hold and that the atmosphere for a Council among Vatican officials is more positive.

In my previous letter I had mentioned some changes in regulations, or the "Regolamento," as the Italian has it. These are changes in the rules of the Council flowing from the experience of the first session. They all aim at a greater efficiency, order and discipline in the way the general meetings will be conducted. For example, among those rules are mentioned the auditors, or laypersons, the first to be invited to any council of the Church. These laypeople will now have the right to speak before the bishops.

Another big change involves those who will be presiding at our future meetings. Instead of the ten cardinals sitting at the Presidential table, each taking a turn to preside, a new ruling body has been formed. There will be four moderators who have received full authority from the Pope to preside over the Council and to lead the discussions in our general meetings. They will determine what subjects are proper for discussion and they will be able to limit speeches or interventions that are not to the point.

The rules have also simplified our mode of dress. Instead of the cumbersome cope and mitre, we'll be wearing what we call the choir robes; red cassocks, surplice rochette, pectoral cross, and mozzetta, a short kind of cape over which we will wear our pectoral crosses.

Yes, I'm excited about going back to Rome and I'm looking forward to a discussion of all those new documents that are to be presented for debate, review, and final decision. Of special interest is the liturgy as well as that very large and comprehensive document on the Nature of the Church. And, oh yes, the controversial schema on the sources of Revelation. I understand from the Cardinal that the special coordinating committee appointed by the pope in the last session has made excellent progress in reconciling the differences that surfaced so strongly last fall.

Pray for us bishops. I'll be writing to you from Rome.

The Second Session of Vatican Council II

September 29, 1963 - December 2, 1963

October 2, 1963

We're back in Rome and the vast elliptical columns that surround St. Peter's Square stretched out their arms with a special welcome to the bishops of all the world gathering for the opening of the Second Session of Vatican II.

On Sunday, September 29, Pope Paul VI, our new Holy Father, at the end of a beautiful liturgy, solemnly opened the Second Session of the Ecumenical Council of Vatican II. In his greeting to us bishops he reaffirmed the pastoral and ecumenical scope of the Council and gave warm expression to the prophetic vision of his predecessor Pope John XXIII who first called us to Rome to look to the inner reform of our Church.

The Holy Father's speech corresponded to his character as I knew him during the war years when I reported to him on the work of the Catholic Relief Services; serious, intelligent, a man of learning and a man of method and order, he assured us that he would devote all his energies to the work of the Council. He asked that our principal concern be to "examine the intimate nature of the Church." In an exquisitely beautiful expression he reminded us bishops that we have "gathered up the broken thread of the First Vatican Council and by that very fact have removed the fear which was wrongly deduced from that Council, that the pope alone rules and governs the Church without the assistance of his bishops in council."

To the sixty-three non-Catholic observers, who had a place of honor near the main altar of St. Peter's, the Pope spoke "as father and brother," expressing his "deep sadness" at the "prolonged separation" of our Churches.

In that very early part of his sixty-three minute speech, Pope Paul boldly addressed what we knew would provoke controversy in the very first document we would be debating, the subject of collegiality or cooperation between the Pope and his bishops. With obvious reference to the document on the Nature of the Church, he stated: "The Lord is our witness when, at this moment of the second session, we declare to you that in our mind there is no intention of human predominance, no jealousy of exclusive power, but only desire and the will to carry out the divine mandate which makes us, of you and among you, Brothers, the supreme shepherd, and which requires of you that you be his joy and glory, the 'communion of saints,' offering your fidelity, your loyalty, your collaboration."

That was typical of the gentle, loving Cardinal Montini who went on to say, "Now that I have greeted you, let me introduce myself to you and tell you of my dreams for this Council." In words similar to Pope John's, he said that "our task is not merely to guard this precious treasure, our faith, as if we were concerned only with antiquity, but to dedicate ourselves with an earnest will and without fear to that work which our era demands of us . . . let us have due regard for the great question of the unity in one flock of those who believe in Christ . . . let us proclaim Christ to ourselves and to the world around us; Christ our beginning, Christ our life and our guide, Christ our hope and our end."

Sharing those words of our Holy Father with you and as I write them for you here in my room at our Chicago House of Studies, I could not help but feel that while our first session of Vatican II ended last year without producing any concrete final result, this autumn will see the Council move on to make decisions which may be of the greatest import for the Church for generations and centuries to come.

As of now we have received fourteen of the seventeen schemas which are on the agenda of Vatican II. They comprise a total of 550 pages. I'm looking forward eagerly to the discussion of the document on the Nature of the Church. It's called "De Ecclesia." It consists of two sections totaling ninety pages. It takes up subjects where Vatican I left off, like the collegiality of bishops, the internationalization of the offices at the Vatican which are largely staffed by Italians, and the role of bishops' conferences in various countries.

Most of the documents, as I talk with my Episcopal confreres, appear quite satisfactory. Others, like the one on the seminary formation of priests and the one on Catholic schools are in for trouble. The schema on the Theology of the Priesthood leaves something to be desired and Cardinal Meyer plans to speak up on this.

The schema on Ecumenism, our relationship with Protestantism and other religions, is one of the best. It will be a landmark in the history of the Church because of its emphasis on the positive relationship between our churches.

I look forward to a resolution of the debate that divided us on Scripture and Tradition, and of course, to witnessing the finishing touches to the schema on the Liturgy for which the groundwork was laid in that first session. That document on the Liturgy with which we struggled last year, will have to be completed and promulgated and made an integral part of the Church's day-to-day life on every level.

The American bishops are vitally interested in the draft on Religious Liberty. The bishops from behind the Iron Curtain will no doubt show great interest in that subject as well as Protestants, because of the Church's legislation on mixed marriages.

The other issues that round out those seventeen documents include these: Mary, Mother of the Church; bishops and the administration of dioceses; clergy; religious; the lay apostolate; Catholic education; and the communications media, which we touched upon in the first session.

Those meetings last year not only demonstrated the effectiveness of the independence and diversity of thinking among the Council Fathers, but, more importantly, brought the bishops closer together and made them far more aware of the universal character of their office.

A moment ago I said that the decisions at this session may have grave import for the Church of the future. The decisions we make will obviously be of greatest concern to Catholics but not to Catholics alone. We comprise half the world's Christians and Christianity is manifestly the largest of the world's international faiths.

How often I've written in our parish bulletin about the little impact we have as Christians in our own ecclesial world, how ineffective we are on the national level, how forgetful we are of the Gospel imperative: "Go you into the whole world and make disciples of all nations."

In that regard there is a rumor here that a document called Schema 13, the brainchild of Cardinal Suenens of Belgium, a close friend of the Pope, has all the earmarks of moving the Church out into the world.

There is some hope that the Church, as she turns her gaze outwards, shaking off her inclination of defensive introspection, will dialogue with the whole world. I think Pope John had that in mind, as does our present Holy Father. Pope John wrote the encyclical "Pacem in Terris" and aimed this Council toward the goal of unity, and Pope Paul, in his opening remarks emphasized that we must "have due regard for the great question of the unity in one flock of those who believe in Christ, and which Pope John has called the paternal home whose doors are open to all."

October 6, 1963

Rome. Do you know my deepest impression is of all that is happening here these days? Anyone with a sense of history cannot help but be moved by this gathering of bishops from all over the world, from every nation, every color and language, yet professing a common tongue. More than any other assembly in the world, this gathering represents a fixed point, around which the storms of twenty centuries have swirled.

Just imagine, what this Council may mean to you, to your friends, to Protestants, Jews, and non-believers. Here I see a sense of continuity, twenty-one ecumenical councils since the time of Christ; here I see stability in a world of change. Only a handful of heads wear crowns today and the oldest and most secure of them is the triple crown worn by our Holy Father. Lay legislatures and constitutions come and go but the Pope today is working with a body of men that finds precedents and inspiration in the oldest annals of the Church.

Yes, I am filled with awe and expectation and the realization of what it means to be here, a member, however obscure, of the Apostolic hierarchy, and called to the Eternal City to help renew the Church of God.

When I left Rome after the first session of the Council I had a strong feeling that a new epoch in the life of the Church has begun. I came home convinced that the Church is really a community and not just a juridical machine, providing us with laws and regulations. I witnessed the reality, despite my years of worldwide service with our American bishops charitable works, that as a member of the College of Bishops, I bear responsibility for the whole Church and not just for our parish or diocese. What made me eager to want to return for this second session was the discovery that all of us bishops were looking toward a concerted effort in the renewal of the life of worship in the

Church, the unity of all Christians, and the adaptation of the Church to the modern world.

Further than that, in this session, we bishops will have to grapple with Pope John's pastoral and ecumenical vision of the Church's mission, make real that vision in such definite and concrete realities as reform of the Roman curial offices which sought to impede that vision and make of us bishops passive participants.

Last year, I mentioned how our American Conference of Bishops met at our college in Rome to either hear some one of the Council's experts explain a document to us or guide us in our deliberations. The other evening, several of us bishops and a half dozen or so priests from home were discussing the role of our Episcopal Conference in the United States. One of the bishops, long a resident in Rome, emphasized that there was, despite their growth on a national and continental level, not too much enthusiasm for bishops' conferences in Rome. He seemed to indicate that the policy of some Roman officials was, "divide et impera," that is, "to divide and conquer."

If I many interpret that for you: A bishop, in dealing with some problem or seeking some help in Rome, might have less influence as a individual than were he to deal through a conference of bishops. That subject of conferences of bishops may come up in this session when we get around to discussion of the draft document on the pastoral role of bishops.

This example will help you understand what we were talking about that evening. There's a section in the document on the Liturgy, already approved by the bishops last year, that hinges on the issue of the bishops' conferences and their authority. After some debate it was unanimously agreed that the national conference of bishops of a particular country would have the authority to *decide*, for instance, the extent to which the vernacular would be used in the liturgy, and the role of the Vatican would not be to legislate but to *confirm* the decision of the bishops.

One of the bishops, a canon lawyer, told us that was something really new. It was a move toward establishing a middle force between the individual bishop and the central government of the Church. I wonder what implications this will have for the future. What with my travels in various countries, especially in South America, I heard of undue interference of papal representatives like papal nuncios or delegates in affairs of the local Church.

Be sure and understand me correctly. It is not a type of carping that I'm reporting but a problem that hinges on the basic issue of what a bishop is all about. We bishops will need to work out a theology of the episcopacy and its relationship to papal primacy, of the collegiality of bishops, which underlies that whole question of the role of bishops' conferences and their authority vis-a-vis the Vatican.

October 12, 1963

Just before the first session of Vatican II closed last December, a document on the Nature of the Church was given us for discussion. I mentioned in one of my letters last year that this matter of what the Church is all about was part of the unfinished business of Vatican I in 1869. On September 30, the day after Pope Paul solemnly opened this second session of the Council, the bishops took up discussion of the draft document "On the Church."

Much of the morning, however, was spent in housekeeping details. Among those we were told four new moderators would preside over our meetings instead of one of the members of the Presidency of the Council, the ten-minute time limit would be enforced, and that a phone would ring near the speaker's microphone at eight minutes into his speech advising him that he had two minutes to conclude.

On October 1, during our first working meeting of this

session, the draft proposal "On the Nature of the Church" was overwhelmingly accepted by the bishops for detailed discussion.

Cardinal Meyer, Bishop O'Donnell and I arrived at St. Peter's about 8:30 that morning. The three of us stopped at St. Peter's tomb for a brief prayer and went to our individual desks. Like most bishops we needed to search for our new places. Since seating was by seniority, Bishop O'Donnell and I were moved up a few aisles indicating that since last year new bishops were appointed and that other bishops were added who had not been present at the first session of the Council.

The Secretary of the Council, Archbishop Felici, reminded us that the introduction and first two chapters of the document on the Church had been mailed to us at home. He also reported that some 370 amendments had been proposed and urged us to get on with the debate.

Among those amendments the secretary mentioned were a number of the objections we heard last December. The most famous of those criticisms was voiced by a bishop from Belgium who insisted that the document was tainted by clericalism, juridicism, and triumphalism.

A bit of Church history may clarify the bishop's statement for you. A venerable ancient writer and bishop, St. Cyprian, once said: "When God permits me to be in your midst, we will treat in common of the things that have been done, or are to be done, with the respect that we owe one another."

Yet, down the centuries that kind of sharing was not always true. I would suggest that extreme clericalism, that is the dominance of decision-making by the hierarchy and local clergy, followed on the Protestant reformation and was sanctified, to a degree, by the Council of Trent in 1545.

In 1906, the saintly Pope Pius X stated what had been that Church policy this way: "The Church is by its very nature an unequal society; it comprises two categories of person – the pastors and the flock. The hierarchy alone moves and controls, the duty of the multitude is to suffer itself to be governed and to carry out in a submissive spirit the orders of those in control."

I am old enough to remember our Church in America as a church of immigrants. Irish, Italian, Polish, and other priests came with their faithful from the old country. The dominant position that priest held in the homeland was continued in the new country. In 19th century America it was the bishop and priest who protected the faith of their flock from Protestantism and the secular elements of a growing American society. But we're an educated Catholic laity now who want a say in the governance of their Church.

At another level the vast majority of the bishops here are in favor of asserting that the bishops should be more closely associated with the Pope, as the apostles had been associated with St. Peter, in a college or group for the spread and governance of the Church. The schema before us makes no mention of this so-called collegiality of the bishops, but rumor is strong that the subject will come up and be hotly debated. The opposition has it that such a concept will erode the power of the Pope.

I foresee that there will be no lack of drama as we move further into that subject of who makes up the Church of God. There is bound to be dramatic exchange between those who are against modernization, yes, who will even continue to resist continuity of the Council, and those who share Pope John's dream of taking the Church out into the world, bishops, priests and laity together, and turning that world toward Christ.

At our third meeting on Wednesday, October 2, Cardinal Gracias of Bombay, India, summed up beautifully what I have just reported to you about the elements of debate on the Church. He said: "The Church exists in itself but not for itself; it exists for service, not for privilege or domination . . . the Church seeks to expand not as a means of increasing its power, but rather in order to increase the scope of its service."

That same day, Archbishop Camara of Rio de Janeiro, whom I met in my travels for Catholic Relief Services, voiced an opinion that must have been very pleasing to our Lord. He said that the schema should contain a declaration of the Church's concern for and solidarity with the great masses of the poor and suffering people throughout the world.

Today we had the first hint of movement toward a discussion of that concept of collegiality I mentioned earlier. Cardinal Alfrink of the Netherlands, a close friend of our Cardinal, rose to express exception to the phrase "Peter and the Apostles" on the grounds that it implies that Peter was not one of the Apostles. He suggested that it be changed to read: "Peter with other Apostles." He felt that Peter was associated with other members of the apostolic college and that this did not weaken his position or authority.

October 20, 1963

It would be superfluous to say that the atmosphere here is supercharged with rumor. That's hardly a novelty here in this city of sanctified rumor and unsanctified anonymity. The saying here among some of us bishops is, believe all that is reported and preserve your childish innocence, doubt everything and everyone and become even a sadder case than before. I would guess we're going to go through a lot of that as the Council moves on.

Here is an example. Last year we heard that the second session of the Council would begin in June. Well, here it is October, and we're just getting down to business. Another rumor has it that this will be the last session of the Council. Well? I think it is better to settle for the law of averages. Some of the stories you hear are bound to be true, or mostly true. Others, well, just remember you're in Rome.

A bishop from Canada sitting next to me reflected the atmosphere here these days this way: "It may not be that all the bright prospects for unity and reconciliation will be fulfilled, but neither will all the candles lit at the shrine of hope sputter out in the blackness of disappointment." I made him write that down so that I would remember his sage observation.

I was reflecting on all this the other day during one of my walks through the Villa Borghese. As I reached the end of the park and stood at the parapet overlooking a good part of the city, the great dome of St. Peter's in the distance evoked a sense of sharing in an ultimate perfection. The dome is serene beyond any comparable architectural creation, psychologically no less than physically. It exudes qualities of solidity and firmness, an agelessness that is the Church of Christ. It will survive rumor and even the mistakes this Council may bring about.

During the past week we moved in many directions. Interventions on the nature of the Church dominated our discussions. Cardinal Ritter of St. Louis emphasized the thrust for unity which Pope John hoped for, saying that the "Church is a sign and an instrument of union," but he went on to decry, and I failed to get the connection, that "preaching and teaching, while sacred duties, are either poorly done or not fulfilled at all." What I think he was trying to tell us is that preaching, which is a vital part of the priest's teaching office, has, up to now, been neglected.

The other evening I went to a lecture sponsored by the bishops from Germany. Their guest was an expert advisor to the Council, Father Karl Rahner, a Jesuit and one of my favorite theologians. Father Rahner made two points that I feel will become an important part of that schema on the Nature of the Church. He emphasized that a separate document on the Blessed Virgin Mary ought not to be discussed but that since she is one with us among the People of God a chapter about her should be added to the schema on the Church. He also suggested that all Catholics, both clerical and lay, are called to be a holy people even though their position in the Church is different.

Here are some bits and pieces about our discussions over the past week or two. I was surprised to hear Cardinal Spellman of New York, who has done much traveling about the world, speak against the restoration of the permanent diaconate. That subject came up when a good number of the missionary bishops spoke of their needs for help because of the lessening number of priests in their areas. Up to now, deacons were ordained with the intent that they would go on to the priesthood. The permanent deacon is one who, even though married, can be ordained to serve the Church in various capacities. I believe the Cardinal's concern was that restoring this ancient custom might lessen the number of those men entering the seminary to study for the priesthood and be bound by the law of celibacy.

It did not dawn on me that there were no women present at the Council until a bishop spoke about their absence and suggested that some women ought to be invited in as "auditors." At dinner that evening our Cardinal told us that there were some plans in the offing to invite several religious and laywomen to the Council as observers.

That subject of collegiality came up again and again. It would be impossible to describe for you all the different approaches made by Council Fathers on this subject. But to refresh your memories. The concept of collegiality among the bishops and the Pope means that we, the bishops as a whole, in union with the Pope, could act with supreme authority on matters affecting the government of the Church. Bishops opposed to the idea felt that this would impinge on the primacy of the Pope as head of the Church. Those in favor of the concept felt that was not true because collegiality emphasizes the primacy, since there can be no real collegiality among the bishops except in union with the Pope.

Cardinal Meyer, a recognized scripture scholar, capped the discussion when he said that all of Christ's mandates to the Apostles were expressed in the plural. The Apostles, furthermore, acted as a college in the choice of a successor to Judas. Here and elsewhere, he said, the collegiality of the bishops is stated as clearly as is the foundation of the Church on Peter.

On October 8, 9 and 14, we cast our first ballots on the amendments to the Constitution on the Liturgy. As the process went it looked like there would be a successful passage of the entire schema, which would greatly affect the liturgical life of the Church in the future. There is no doubt that the liturgy has to be made less clerical, more ecclesial and more open to participation.

Among those amendments, all of which passed overwhelmingly, were a revision of the Mass which would give greater simplicity to the Mass and avoid duplication of certain parts which have been added to it over the centuries; the sermon, now called the homily, would be required at every Mass at which there is a congregation; lay participation in the Mass and liturgical education to make the Mass, the sacraments and sacramentals, all of the Church's public prayer better understood; the use of the vernacular languages in the Mass, so thoroughly debated, was a history-making decision that I feel you will like. I should tell you that the wording in the schema says that the vernacular *may be used;* the use of Latin is to be retained.

There's a beautiful sentence in that schema on the liturgy. It goes like this: "The Church, when it is not a question of the faith or the common good, does not intend to impose, even in the liturgy, a rigid uniformity. Moreover, it requests and promotes the characteristics and gifts of the various races and peoples. It looks favorably on everything in the customs of these people that is not bound up with superstition and error, and, if it can it protects and conserves them."

May I emphasize that while we were moving ahead with our votes on the liturgy documents, the debates on the Nature of the Church schema continued. I'll get back to those.

Other amendments to the Liturgy schema included concelebration of Mass when two or more priests are present rather than separate Masses at individual altars; the extension of the use of the vernacular to the sacraments and sacramentals; changed the name of the sacrament of Extreme Unction to that of the Anointing of the Sick. If you want the numbers, 2,239 bishops voted for those changes and there were only 42 against them. And yes, communion under both species, bread and wine, was approved. It is interesting that certain sacramentals could be administered by laypersons. I think this will become quite the general practice when the order of the permanent diaconate is approved. I can also foresee those deacons witnessing marriages, baptizing, counseling in marriage preparation courses, working in hospitals, etc.

October 26, 1963

As this great Council settles down to the orderly routine of its sessions, this might be the time to tell you something about the arrangements there. One just has to marvel and pay tribute to the extraordinary foresight that went into the physical preparations for this meeting of the world's bishops. The public address system, despite the vastness of the nave of St. Peters, is phenomenal. The only complaint one hears has to do with the cramped space given each of us to work with those large folio size schemas or documents. One of them takes up almost all of the space on my little desk with little room for writing notes. But then how else could you crowd in almost three thousand bishops.

Serving the more practical function of waiting on the

bishops, collecting their votes, distributing the various documents, carrying messages, finding a lost pen or pencil, are a variety of seminarians selected with an eye and ear to their ability to speak the various languages. However, English is the tongue most commonly understood by the bishops, sometimes haltingly, but with a mixture of Italian or French.

But I must tell you of the treat we get in listening to the Sistine Choir at the celebration of daily Mass before our working sessions begin. These are Low Masses, offered by bishops from every corner of the world, and answered in dialogue form by the whole body of the Council Fathers present. During the quiet intervals of the Mass, the Offertory, the Canon, and the Communion, the choir, with the benefits of that extraordinary sound system, sings the compositions of the supreme masters of Church music. I'm sure that before this Council is over we will have heard the whole cycle of Palestrina's motets, rendered with superb finish and understanding.

I learned from my British neighbor the full name of that famous 16th century Church-music genius, and it intrigued me because of my first name: Joannes Petraloysius Praenestinus. I looked this up at our college. Palestrina, while wholly absorbed in the subtle intricacies of polyphonic music, was always aware that the purpose of Church music was not only sound but meaning, not only counterpoint but prayer.

And so it is that over the heads of the Conciliar Fathers, graying or already white for the most part, float each morning of our sessions the glorious strains of an artist who four centuries ago conceived the glory of God in the grandeur of music. And that did not escape us bishops, because in the schema on the Liturgy we gave considerable time to the proper use of music at Mass and other ceremonies of public worship.

But back to work. A significant by-product of our discussions on the Nature of the Church and the role of bishops in that matter of collegiality, or shared responsibility, was the suggestion by a bishop from England that there ought to be a group of bishops, selected from throughout the world, who would assist the Pope in the government of the universal Church. Later on I heard the expression: "A Synod of Bishops" ought to be setup to work with the Pope when the Council comes to an end.

Perhaps I ought to clarify the concept of power and structure that seeps into our conversations here. It will, I feel, have a lot to do with the way the Church will be run universally and even in our parishes. There is the view of the Church that comes to us from what our Lord said to St. Peter: "You are Peter, the rock, and upon that rock I will build my Church." That is the Church as we see it headed by the Pope. The Pope stands, as it were, at the summit of a pyramid, and from him the bishops and clergy derive their sacred powers to be used in serving the people who form the base of the pyramid.

The other view begins with the notion that the Church is the Great Assembly, the People of God, called by Him into His family. To minister and to guide this people Christ initiated a hierarchy at whose head stands the Pope. In this view the various offices in the Church of bishop, priest and deacon are seen as ministries to meet the needs of the people.

The problem we're having here in Rome is where the emphasis should lie. At lunch the other day, Father John Courtney Murray, the highly respected American theologian, said that as a body we bishops are searching within ourselves to find and express the Church's consciousness of herself, and that the laity ought to make the same effort. He felt that the consciousness of Church was present in our immigrant Church in America but over the generations the image of the Church as the People of God was dimmed or obscured.

Following our discussions on the hierarchical nature of the Church, something you might find too technical to understand, there followed a debate about the role of laity, the fourth chapter of our document. This will be the first time in the history of the 21 Ecumenical Councils that the topic of the role of the laity in the Church will be the subject of debate.

The schema treats the role of the laity in the Church and builds on the liturgy document which states that through participation in the Mass it is easier for Christians to realize that they are the Church that Christ associates with himself in the exercise of his priesthood. The document goes as far as to say that the laity could "supply sacred functions." Given that type of ministry, laypersons would not only be lectors, or readers of the sacred scriptures at Mass, but even distributors of Holy Communion.

The language in the schema is very interesting in this regard. "The laity have the capacity of being appointed to some ecclesiastical offices with a view to a spiritual end." It will be interesting to see how prophetic those words are in the future.

Here is a definition of the laity as we are beginning to study your role in the Church: "The laity are members of the People of God who are distinct from priests and religious, but who are incorporated into Christ through Baptism and thus share in their own way in his priestly, prophetic and kindly office, exercising the mission of the whole Christian people in the Church and in the world."

Primarily, the document states that the specific characteristic of the laity is that they are secular, out in the world, and their vocation is that of seeking the kingdom of God in the administration of temporal things by directing them toward God. And secondly, they may be appointed to exercise certain "sacral functions" or ministries in the Church.

Part of the mission of the layperson is not only to listen to the word of God, but also to be co-responsible with the priest in the preaching and exercising of the Christian message. The old concept of the layperson as one "who prays, pays and obeys," is no longer tenable according to Bishop Primeau, a classmate of mine from Chicago, who mentioned that phrase on the floor of St. Peter's.

That idea of collegiality between the bishops and the Pope is also applicable here. The schema, in speaking of the laity's relationship to bishop and priest, emphasizes that you have the right to expect care and assistance from the "pastors of the Church." The laity also has the duty to assist them in their work. I foresee calling upon you for greater cooperation in the administration of our parish back home. One of my bishop neighbors here put it bluntly this way: "It's about time the laity carried their load for the mission of the Church."

A bishop from France put it all in a nutshell when he said: "Too many Christians seek the spiritual security and personal satisfaction in their reception of the sacraments without ever experiencing the practical consequences of incorporation into the Mystical Body of Christ." So it's not just Church on Sunday but involvement with the Church's mission every day.

October 30, 1963

Walking is the best way to see Rome. On the weekends it is interesting to drop in on those various churches in Rome, large ones and the smaller ones tucked away on some side street. Most are dark, poorly lighted, have no pews, but there's always a side chapel with chairs where the Blessed Sacrament is reserved. They are quiet places where one can rest and shut out the din of Roman traffic.

One of the Italian bishops told me that about 30% of the Roman women attend Mass, and some 10% of the men. Out in the suburbs, especially up in the Alban hills where I go to visit a priest whom I helped through the seminary, attendance is much like at home – around 80%, with a good mixture of men and women. Father Gaetano, the pastor, named his new church, built by the government, after our own church of Immaculate Heart of Mary. He lives next door in a new rectory with his mother and sister; it's his way of supporting them.

At the moment, of course, Rome is enjoying the presence of so many bishops who are adding a great deal to the local economy. It's hard to tell whether the Romans have a grasp of the importance of what we're trying to do in the Council. They do, however, love the pageantry that is part of our lives here. Walking the narrow by-ways, one gets a whiff of what a French writer said was "Le Parfum de Rome." Most often that whiff comes from a little deli tucked between stores that is ready to serve you a fresh cup of "cappuccino," coffee steamed with milk. Or, sometimes it's the smell of that evening's dinner being prepared for those coming home from work or school. And, of course, Italians love flowers.

Yesterday, I found my way to the numbered seat assigned to me at the beginning of this session of the Council. As I moved up the stairs to the ninth tier I saluted those assigned around me and with whom I built up the intimacy of small jokes shared, idiosyncrasies acknowledged, prejudices confessed. It is impossible to sit next to a man through all these sessions of some three hours apiece without coming to learn a good deal about him. You soon learn that you have been placed between a biblical scholar and a theologian, a bishop from a developed country like ours and a black bishop from Africa eager to tell you how the Church is growing and what dreams he has for it as a result of the Council.

One of the bishops from England near me remarked "isn't it great how this Council brings forth the Church's treasures." He was referring to the priceless value of the minds that are getting together here, how barriers are bro-

A typical gathering of Bishops in the after hours of a session of the Council. In this instance, several American Bishops meet with Bishops from Poland and others who were able to get to the Council from behind the Iron Curtain. The author is seen standing next to the future Pope John Paul II.

ken down, and how that sense of hierarchy becomes real.

And so, we begin another session, maybe a sparkling one or a wearisome one, but certainly revelatory of the creative minds that are at work here these days.

Last Thursday, that would be the 25th, the bishops voted to close discussion of the schema "On the People of God and the Laity." That opened up other areas in the schema on the Nature of the Church. The separate schema on the Blessed Virgin Mary came up for brief discussion and it appears that the schema might become a chapter in the larger document on the Church. A bishop from Poland, Karol Wojtyla of Krakow, expressed what seems to be the feeling of most bishops, that the opening chapter of the schema on the Church should be "On the People of God."

Our Cardinal Meyer spoke on the subject also but added that the schema "should not speak only of the privileges of the people of God, but should emphasize very strongly the difficulties of leading a genuinely Christian life."

I should mention that when dealing with the subject of the married diaconate, the matter of celibacy for priests came up again and again. One of the Council experts stated that, "celibacy is not a divine law, but a disciplinary law of the Church which could be changed." I have a feeling that the Holy Father is going to have to state his position on this delicate matter.

A week ago Friday the bishops began discussion of the fourth chapter of the schema on the Church, "The Call to Holiness" that applies to all the People of God. The chapter contains a beautiful description of that call whatever a person's state in life. It does not make reference to religious who are bound by vows to seek holiness in their lives, and bishops, priests and deacons as well. The obligation of married people to set an example of holiness for their children was emphasized.

Last Tuesday, the 29th, the bishops voted to include the schema on our Blessed Lady as a chapter in the document on the Church rather than in a separate schema. The vote was evenly divided. Those opposed to the idea felt that our Lady's glory would be diminished.

I ought to report to you that bishops often rose to speak about the separation of Church and State. Those bishops from behind the Iron Curtain felt quite strongly about including some language on that subject in the schema on the Church. We Americans were as firm in pushing for a clear statement on religious liberty. At an evening meeting we had at the North American College there was talk of preparing a separate schema on Religious Liberty. True, there is a chapter on that subject in the schema on Ecumenism springing from the problems we've had in interfaith relationship but, in the opinion of our own Cardinal and other experts on the subject, such inclusion obscures the more general treatment of religious liberty as an affirmation of the dignity of the human person that consists essentially in his freedom.

In other words, a separate document would apply to more than our American problems in this regard. Other countries, where totalitarian governments posed a threat to human freedom, would join an American move in support of such a document.

I can report that the Council Fathers voted overwhelmingly to give bishops a larger role in governing the Church and to restore the ancient order of deacons. Today the Council's work seemed to be quickening. Discussions on the schema on the Church are coming to an end and it is our hope that by the time we end this session that schema will be passed and presented to the Holy Father for approval and promulgation.

November 5, 1963

In one of my letters I mentioned that on our way to Rome by ship we docked in Palermo, Sicily for a day. Cardinal Ruffini, the Archbishop of that island, is a longtime friend of Cardinal Meyer. We truly enjoyed the company of these two great scripture scholars. This morning Cardinal Ruffini gave a press conference which was enlightening. He has a wry sense of humor. In his eyes, priests are officers and laypersons, an extension of the clergy, are second-class soldiers. The Church needs them "to go to the front and conquer the enemy. What would officers do if they had no soldiers under their command?" he asked.

The Cardinal also felt that laypeople are important because they hold key positions in the secular world; in the press, in the movie industry, television, in universities, schools, and in politics. They must influence these positions for good, for the elimination of devastating materialism. He said we need, among the laity, martyrs and witnesses to the faith.

It seems that this Council will mark a historic turning point in the apostolic life of the Church. The relatively untapped talents and energies of lay Catholics will at long last be channeled into the mainstream of the Church's mission and work. The age of the lay apostolate has arrived. The liturgy document we passed the other day, and now waiting approval by the Holy Father, is the opening of the door to that apostolate. The laity will be advising bishops on the diocesan level as well as the pastor on the parochial level.

One the Cardinals, Doepfner of Munich, complained about the slow pace of the Council's deliberations. I would agree with him. We Americans and the Germans like to put in a full days work. It's almost 10:30 AM by the time Mass is ended and we begin our actual work. Then the day ends by 1:30 PM. True, we do have our meetings in the late afternoon and evenings, but it seems such a waste of time to bring almost two thousand bishops together for just a few hours. Basically, one of the problems is that some bishops exceed the time limit for speeches, then there are those who make speeches just to be heard or to be on the record for posterity.

Cardinal Doepfner was applauded for his statement.

After that, discussion continued on the chapter that had to do with the "Call to Holiness in the Church." Criticism was raised because the chapter did not spell out the practical steps necessary to achieve holiness. I did not think that was necessary. You, for instance at home, have heard much from the pulpit regarding devotions and other means to acquire holiness. Then there are the sacraments and their primacy of grace in the achievement of holiness. In a nutshell, this chapter on holiness is meant to emphasize that all of us, not just the clergy and religious are called to holiness.

During the past week we began debating the schema "On Bishops and the Government of Dioceses," a subject that brought to the fore that ticklish situation of our relationships with the Curia, or the Pope's office in Rome. The document also contains sections that relate to the role of auxiliary bishops, something of interest to me; the resignation of bishops because of age and illness; Episcopal conferences and the division of dioceses. It is almost impossible to summarize the discussion of this document because of the variety of theoretical and practical aspects.

Again, collegiality came up. A French bishop put it well when he said that the practical exercise of collegiality demands that individual bishops have a direct share in the solution of church problems. I have a feeling that this matter of better cooperation between the bishops and Rome will come up again and again.

Remember, I mentioned that decisive vote on October

30th when the Council Fathers voted overwhelmingly to give bishops a larger role in governing the Church. That decisive vote puts the theological language of sharing responsibilities in this way: Every bishop, who is in union with all the bishops and the Pope, belongs to the body or college of bishops. That college of bishops succeeds the college of the Apostles and, together with the Pope, has full and supreme power over the whole Church.

The bishops are loyal to the Holy Father and love him. It's simply a matter of our desire to share more intimately the responsibilities he has to govern the Church.

November 18, 1963

By now you must surmise that bishops are human and do have their own eccentricities. It would be foolish to deny that there are differences of opinion here, theological and procedural, sometimes expressed with considerable vigor and determination. But that was to be expected especially when the bishops in that very first meeting in 1962 declared their independence of thinking from that of the curial officials who, so to speak, tried to "stack the deck." Hope you are not scandalized. The Holy Spirit is with us and will in the end strongly and sweetly bring all things into harmony.

There is complete freedom of debate, limited of course, by the bounds of orthodoxy. As a matter of fact, the debates I witness are marked by a good bit of balance, poise and good temper, even some humor now and then. The other day one of the bishops, in talking about "The Call to Holiness," suggested that holiness was not being encouraged by those who "run the sainthood office" since so many Italians become saints and so few in other parts of the world. With tongue in cheek he said "why can't we dig up the dry bones of our own people and make saints out of them; maybe we need that example."

I must confess that the Council has been a great opportunity for me to brush up on the Latin I learned and used in the seminary. Now and then I am thrilled to catch the nuances of that language when some bishop knows how to use the beauty of Latinity. But then again, Latin with a Spanish or French accent is hard to understand and that's when things get dull and bishops share their doodling masterpeices with each other.

But there are bishops sitting near me with rapt faces, clearly drinking in the elegance of another bishop's speech; and there are those who nod and smile their accord with the speaker, whether or not they understand the subtleties of the theological point the speaker is trying to get across. And there are bishops who shake their heads and frown, obviously displeased and full of indignation that anyone could be so wrong or take up our time with such nonsense.

And there are times, when on our way to the college, the Cardinal would ask if we agreed with one or another of the bishops. Once I said, "Your Eminence, I missed the point of that speech, and I nodded now and then." Then came that gentle reprimand: "How late did you men stay out last night?"

Tomorrow, the Cardinal told us, the subject of religious liberty will come up in connection with the discussion of the schema on "Ecumenism." Pope John XXIII insisted that Christian Unity was to be at the heart of this Council. With that, we touch one of the most sensitive nerves of modern religious life, especially in our country. With all those observers of various faith in listening in on us, I wonder what direction we will take. Everyone here knows that in treating of Christian Unity, Vatican II is handling a delicate key to the future of Christianity.

My English neighbor, half in jest said: "We'll soon learn whether Pope John was right in making ecumenism the principal issue of Vatican II." One of the Cardinals in presenting the schema to us for discussion said: "Let us be under no illusion. Union will not be achieved quickly, but at least we must open and not close the doors."

From my own experience during the war years when I worked with members of the other churches to bring refuge and relief to the victims of that war, I learned much about what we have in common rather than what divides us. I hope this Council walks in that direction.

Cardinal Ritter of St. Louis made the first reference to the subject of religious liberty, and probably having our own country in mind, said, "The very liberty of the act of faith demands total independence from all civil power." Later, when I ran into several of the bishops from Poland, they told me how moved they were by that sentence. I need not tell you why.

November 25, 1963

Having lived in the Middle East for several years and having witnessed the birth of the Jewish state of Israel, I was not surprised to hear a number of the bishops from that part of the world object strongly to any discussion of Jews in the schema on "Ecumenism." The fourth chapter of that document is titled, "The Attitude of Catholics Towards Non-Christians and Particularly Toward the Jews."

The opening salvo, a week ago, was provided by a Syrian Rite Patriarch who said: "Neither the Jews nor religious liberty should be treated in the schema." I would agree on the religious liberty issue since the Americans here would prefer a separate document; as for the Jewish question, perhaps that too should be treated separately. In any case, the text as it stood, because of the political situation in the Middle East, did engender confusion, to say the least.

The Cardinal Archbishop of Palermo, Italy was quite direct. He felt that if there is to be a discussion of the Jews, then other religions, less hostile to the Church than the

Jews, should be given preference since they would be more open to conversion to the Catholic faith. An archbishop from Egypt, understandably, wanted no part of the Jewish problem in the text. "Why should this Council issue a statement on anti-Semitism?" he asked.

Cardinal Bea, the scholarly and gentile, German-born head of the commission that prepared the document on ecumenism, inspired more than two thousand bishops into silence and rapt attention when he said: "Jews are not to be made scapegoats for the crucifixion of Christ. The statement on the anti-Semitism is purely religious in nature and there is no question of the Council involving itself in Arab-Israeli politics. We should stand firm, in the light of the Christian principles of justice and love, for the people who gave humanity the Savior."

One of the experts and advisors to the Council told us that inclusion of Jews in the "Ecumenism" schema was justified because the "roots of the Church are in Israel; the Church is grafted in Israel." He went on to say that "the division produced in the people of Israel, between those who accepted Christ as the Messiah and those who did not, is a symbol of all subsequent divisions within the Christian people themselves." A priest, long a staff member of the Office for Promoting Christian Unity, informed us that inclusion of the Jews in the ecumenism text was the specific request of Pope John XXIII.

While appreciating the feelings of the bishops from the Middle East, most of the bishops moved to recognition of the divisions that existed among Christians and felt that we should not be afraid to admit the faults of the past or to ask pardon if need be of our separated brethren.

With only a few days to go before the closing of this session of the Council on December 4th, there is concern that some of the more controversial topics we handled are purposely being held up in commission. But something is being done about that. Pope Paul has ordered a reorganization of the Council Commissions by increasing their membership with more objective people, and again, in order to forestall the delaying tactics I just mentioned. The Pope will name one of the additional members and the bishops will vote on the others.

On the 19th, Bishop De Smet of Bruges, Belgium presented the "relatio" or introductory remarks on the chapter on Religious Liberty in the Ecumenism document. His speech was one of the high points of this session and was remarkable for its clarity, sincerity, and conviction.

At one of our socials with some bishops friends I learned that Father Murray, whom I mentioned before, and who was sitting at the other end of the room, had a hand in the writing of the chapter on religious liberty. Provoked into giving his view of the last chapter in the ecumenism document, Father Murray explained that this chapter is best understood in the light given it by Bishop De Smet when he introduced the chapter on the floor of St. Peter's. Here are some of the reasons the bishop gave why the chapter must be debated by the Council Fathers:

The Church must teach and defend the right to religious liberty since it is a question of truth. So much of the world today is deprived of religious liberty by the atheistic materialism. The Church cannot stand by, nor can the Church leave herself open to the charge that she fosters religious liberty only in those situations where she is the majority religion.

The next morning, the General Secretary of the Council announced that a vote would be taken relative to discussion of the first three chapters on the schema on "Ecumenism" but that chapters IV and V, on the Jewish question and religious liberty, would be voted on at another time. Everyone wondered why the last two chapters would be eliminated from such a vote.

Consternation broke out and I noticed that Cardinal Meyer had approached the desk where the moderators of the Council sat and seemed to be engaged in a lively conversation with one of them. Out of curiosity, Bishop O'Donnell and I made our way to the front of the tiers of seats and by the time we reached the Cardinal he was surrounded by other bishops.

Sure enough, the truth was out. The Presidency of the Council on which the Cardinal served was not consulted about a delay in voting on the Religious Liberty subject. One of the bishops suggested to the Cardinal that a paper be circulated among the bishops asking for signatures to a petition that would go to the Holy Father seeking his intervention that we take a vote.

That evening at the college, the Cardinal told us that the morning's fiasco could have been avoided had the Secretary spelled out the real reasons for the delaying vote on Religious Liberty. It appeared that Cardinal Bea, the head of the Secretariat for Christian Unity, sought an appeal to a vote in order not to rush things through on so controversial a matter in the last days of our meetings.

Later indeed, the Pope indicated his displeasure with the way the Religious Liberty issue was handled. He instructed the dean of the College of Cardinals to announce to us that, indeed, the chapter on religious liberty would be open for discussion by the Council and that it would have first consideration on the agenda at the next session of the Council.

November 22nd will be another day recorded into the history of Vatican II. The schema on the Liturgy providing sweeping reform on the way we pray and worship was passed by the Council Fathers with only 19 dissenting votes out of a total 2,178 votes cast. That action was greeted with prolonged applause and justified Pope John XXIII's desire that Liturgy be the first of the documents of Vatican II because of its pastoral implications.

The Decree on Communications and the Media, a few days later, joined that of the Liturgy as another piece of work completed by the Ecumenical Council.

As for the rest of the closing days of November we delved into such matters as the validity of mixed marriages before non-Catholic ministers, permission to attend non-Catholic religious services and participation with non-Catholics in religious studies.

Just as I was making my way back to my place, after a coffee break, I heard one of the bishops insisting that we should emphatically disapprove of mixed marriages entirely. However, he insisted that if such marriages take place we should insist on religious schools for the education of the children in such marriages, and if the non-Catholic party refuses to bring up the children in the Catholic faith, the marriage should be called off. That reminded me of my first appointment as a priest in a parish where the pastor absolutely refused to let us assistants witness mixed marriages.

On the 29th, the 78th meeting of Vatican II, we were told that the third session of the Council was set for September 14 to November 20, 1964.

December 4, 1963

At the last meeting of the second session of the Council on December 2nd, the Secretary, Bishop Felici, announced on behalf of the Holy Father that prior to the next session, the commissions would meet frequently in order to expedite the work of the Council. We were urged, that despite the responsibilities of our dioceses, we study the documents we would be getting and send in our observations.

The beloved Cardinal Bea, whom I mentioned before, was one of the last speakers to address us on that closing day. He not only thanked us for those positive votes on the first three chapters of the document on Ecumenism but urged us to study the last two chapters on Jews and Religious Liberty in these words: "The questions treated in those chapters remain entrusted to your study and examination during the months to come. You will be smothered in work when you get home, but please, give serious attention to those chapters and send me your observations by the end of February."

On the 4th, the Holy Father celebrated the solemn closing of this session of the Council. In his farewell he told us that he would be making a pilgrimage to the Holy Land in January. He also hinted that he hoped the next session of the Council would be the last. On our flight home some of us bishops, given the unfinished work of the Council, wondered if that would be possible.

In my next letter or two I will be trying to summarize for you what I think this second session of Vatican II accomplished. It seems to me that much more needs to be done and it may be that the Holy Father forgot what he said when he took over the leadership of the Council after Pope John's death. Then he said: "Many of the Council's results have not yet come to maturity, but they are grains of wheat cast into the furrows awaiting their effective and fruitful development in the future."

On the 4th the Holy Father celebrated the solemn closing of this session of the Council. His announcement of approval and promulgation of the Constitution on the Sacred Liturgy brought forth a tremendous burst of applause. In his talk the Pope told us that he would be making a pilgrimage to the Holy Land in January. He also expressed the wish that the Council end with the third session next fall. He announced that on February 16, 1964, the first Sunday of Lent, instructions would be sent to the bishops on how to implement the changes in the liturgy.

You will probably be witnessing that closing of the second session of Vatican II on television so there would be no point in my describing its grandeur. The Italian paper in describing that solemnity stated that besides the 2,000 plus bishops in St. Peter's, there were at least 10,000 people packed into the church. Tomorrow, I will return to St.

Peter's Square for a last goodbye. As the bishops fly or sail or take the train they will be asking themselves the self-same questions they themselves will be asked by curious laity and busy reporters when they arrive home. On that long flight home, I too will be rehearsing answers.

In my next letter or two I will be trying to summarize for you what I think this second session of Vatican accomplished. Much more remains to be done and the Pope in his talk expressed that best when he said: "Many of the Council's results have not yet come to maturity, but they are grains of wheat cast into the furrows awaiting their effective and fruitful development in the future."

Between Second Session and Third Session

December 9, 1963 - September 14, 1964

December 9, 1963

Now that I'm home and ready to catch up with the needs of our parish and the diocese I'd like you to know that I spent yesterday, the Feast of the Immaculate Conception, in a review of our work at the Second Session of Vatican II. Consider this review as a foundation for the reports that I will share with you later, of that homework the Holy Father urged us to attend to before we return to Rome in the fall.

Overall, as I look back over the past few months, I saw real development and growth among the bishops, in the consciousness of what Pope John XXIII wanted of the Council – an updating of the Church and an invitation to you, the laity, to join your bishops, priests and religious in a pastoral and religious adaptation of the message of Christ to the needs of our times.

It is true that the record of actual accomplishment, in the sense of schemas discussed and amended and voted upon, was small. The documents on the Church, the Episcopate and the Government of Dioceses were merely touched upon. But they'll be resurrected as soon as we return to Rome next fall. Personally I'm looking forward to studying the schema on Divine Revelation – the sources of the sacred scriptures, a debate in the third session. We were promised that the schema on Communications got through but I'm afraid it will have little impact. The phrase, "Rome was not built in a day," has application here because I can hardly imagine the Vatican changing its long-established policy of making available to us bishops information before it gets to the media.

We should remember that it is characteristic of the secular press to seek the sensational because that sells papers. The media tried so hard to learn why in the same Church there are progressives and conservatives, those who are forging ahead of the times and those who would lag behind out of love and respect for the venerable past. The press found it hard to understand, and therefore there was no "news" to report about bishops who addressed their brothers in quiet courtesy. Yet, that was the ordinary diet in all our sessions. I'm afraid that some of the media people forgot that this was a meeting of Christians, even if they are bishops.

Perhaps what stood out very happily in the second session of the Council was the unanimity among the bishops. That became evident in the majorities reached during the voting process on the schemas. We ironed out our differences in the first session and applied the new knowledge to the work of our second meeting. The conservative minds of the first session gave way to the "opening of windows" Pope John hoped for in calling us to Vatican II. As a result there may be more freedom and more action in the Church of the future.

Through all those long hours of discussion we bishops became familiar with the conciliar process. We, maybe to the surprise of some bishops, recognized that the Roman Catholic Church was no longer a Mediterranean Church dominated by the bishops of that area of the world; no longer a West-European, or more so, a South European Church, but a worldwide Church where every people, race and tongue had a say in its government.

I sincerely feel that it was providential that our first session started with the Constitution on the Sacred Liturgy, and that the second session ended with its almost unanimous approval and promulgation by the Holy Father. What remains is a concerted effort by everyone to put that beautifully worded document into practice. Much needs to be taught and learned about the way we will worship and pray in the future.

Liturgy is the external expression of worship, its embodiment in action, words, gestures, song, and symbol. Of its very nature it must be formal; it can never allow itself to descend to the merely haphazard or the improvised. It needs also to be repetitive, to say and do the same things over and over again. The best example I can give you are in the very words of the consecration of the bread and wine into the Body and Blood of Christ. Christ gave us those words and their repetition with absolute fidelity has not diminished their meaning.

Despite the liturgical changes I've written to you about, the same Mass will still be offered. The essential elements have not been changed by Vatican II despite the criticisms of some groups in our country who insist that unless it is in Latin, it is not the same Mass. Unless it's the Latin Mass of the Council of Trent, the Mass of St. Pius V, it is no Mass.

Pope Paul VI, with undiminished authority, writes, in ordering the Mass of Vatican II: "What we have prescribed in this Apostolic Constitution shall begin to be in force on the First Sunday of Advent this year, November 30. We decree that these laws and prescriptions be firm and effective now and in the future, **notwithstanding, to the extent necessary, the apostolic constitutions and ordinances issued by our predecessors.**"

The shift to the vernacular – English, French, German, Polish, Chinese, Swahili, or what have you, the abbreviation of the offertory, and the addition of new canons, have in no way affected a change in the basic meaning and thrust of the Mass. We may, at some future date, regret some of those modifications because of misuse, (regret, for instance, the poor translations into English) but it is non-sense to say that the Mass of Vatican II is no longer the Mass of our Lord's institution.

December 18, 1963

My last letter to you ended with a strong defense of the changes in the Mass that will go into effect on the first Sunday of Lent on February 16, 1964. This letter and several more will be an attempt to prepare you for those changes and familiarize you with the thinking of your bishops who followed Pope John's suggestion that "we get in step with the times."

The celebration of the liturgy is, after all, the principal manifestation of the Church, and since the bishops gathered for Vatican II would be primarily concerned with Church, the liturgy would naturally be the first order of business.

The Constitution on the Liturgy is eminently **pastoral,** i.e., the bishops' major concern in writing it was to see that their flocks – you the faithful of our dioceses and parishes – would be better nourished; the goal is participation with understanding. It is also **evangelical,** in the sense that it is framed throughout in the spirit, and often the very words of the gospel. It is **theological,** because in no way is it our intention to ask that you do something without giving you sound theological reasons why the Church worships as she does. And finally, that constitution is **juridical,** but never just that. It has the force of law without unduly venerating the concept of law. The life-infusing spirit of Christ is there giving meaning to all law for Christians who understand the law of love.

With regard to all the changes that will be coming in the Mass, as well as other sacraments, there's an important paragraph in the liturgy document you may want to remember that says: "The liturgical rites should express more clearly the holy things which they signify; the faithful should be enabled to understand them with ease and take part in them fully, actively and as befits a community."

A bit of history will help. After the Council of Trent in 1545 our Church entered on a period of some three and a half centuries during which no real development of the liturgy took place. It was a long period of changelessness and rubricism. The result was that a gulf occurred between people in Church and those entrusted with the celebration of the Mass. Rubricism, strict adherence to laws and regulations, discouraged genuine participation of the people in what was the public prayer of the Church – the Mass.

A liturgical movement for change began about fifty years ago in France, Belgium and the United States, especially by the Benedictine monks. They sought change not for the sake of change, but urged adaptation of the Mass and other religious rites to meet modern conditions and modern requirements. The key word was participation.

I emphasize that language, or more formally, the vernacular, was not the essential principle we bishops were thinking about in the Council when it came to changes in the Mass and other sacraments, but **participation.** Our thought was to eliminate the unnecessary opposition between public and private prayer. The first chapter of the liturgy constitution emphasizes that.

Given that fact, it follows that you who come to Mass must come to it with proper dispositions, that your minds should be attuned to what goes on in the liturgy. Your priest should be mindful that more is required of him than mere observation of the laws; he must also be properly disposed to celebrate Mass. You, the laity, must be given the opportunity to take part in the Mass and be enriched by its effects in your life.

What does that mean? Well, private prayer is also very necessary, but it should harmonize with the liturgical life of the Church. It means that long-standing habits both among priests and people must be changed. For instance, the rosary has its place in our lives, as a private devotion, but not while Mass is going on.

Here is another principle that may cause some disturbance. The Constitution says that the liturgy "should be adapted to the culture and traditions of nations." I can visualize Mass being celebrated quite differently, although the essentials are the same, in our country, yes, even in different parts of it. Black people have their culture, and ways of celebrating, this includes the Mass; the Spanish people, a large part of our population in the Southwest, and various ethnic groups coming from other countries have carried their traditions to this land of the free.

Imagine the new liturgy of the Mass in China, Africa, the Islands of the South Pacific. We celebrated Mass during the Council with a black archbishop from Africa who wore what we Westerners thought were outlandish vestments. He was accompanied with tom toms and songs in his native tongue. By the way, the Chinese prefer white to black for their funerals.

There will be a real revolution in Catholic worship all over the world. Principles that were overlaid with excessive ritualism will be radically altered. The liturgy will, at long last, find its proper place in the life of the Church and no longer be seen or experimented as a private celebration by the priest. The vernacular is in, but Latin is not out. Just remember that the Council Fathers emphasized **participation,** a participation that is full, conscious, and active.

December 23, 1963

In two days we'll be celebrating our Christmas liturgies in Latin for the last time, with our splendid choir doing all the singing and your priest most of the praying. Those of you who have adapted to some of the early liturgical changes introduced by Pope Pius XII, will have your Latin-

English missal on hand. You will follow silently the actions and words of your priest, acknowledging his greeting of "Dominus Vobiscum" with your "Et cum spiritu tu tuo."

I know that my dad will be at St. Michael's with his large print private prayer book, repeating the prayers he's been saying over many years. And when his eyes tire, he will take to the rosary and only allow the sermon to interrupt his Sunday worship. I wonder what he will say to me after February 16th when the new liturgy of the Mass will be implemented in our archdiocese.

Dad is so much like the elderly people of our parish community, set in their ways. I worry about the delicate task of instructing him and them in the new ways of the liturgy. I cringe about telling them about the new rite of confession. It will be called the rite of reconciliation, and there will be the choice of confessing our sins to our priests face to face or behind a screen. I've a suspicion Dad and his elderly confreres have so little to hide they will go for it.

January 4, 1964

Sure enough, my dad had a lot of questions about the changes in the Liturgy the Church will be introducing on the first Sunday of Lent this year. So by way of instruction, I plan to devote the next few letters to those changes.

Remember, **participation** is the key word for the way we'll be celebrating Mass in the future as well as in the way we approach the other sacraments. The popular stress has been on the vernacular, the use of English, but the fact of the matter is your bishops at the Council of Vatican II stressed participation as the key change in the liturgy. That was, as will be with so many other matters of Church policy and practice, what Pope John desired of the Council – "aggiornamento," getting in step with the times.

My dad asked, as will many of his generation, why the changes? I told him the reasons were spelled out in the very introduction of the Constitution on the Sacred Liturgy. One, to impart a greater intensity of Christian life; two, the adaptation of changeable institutions to contemporary Christian needs; three, the ultimate unity of all Christians; and, four, the spread of the gospel.

"Not good enough," my dad replied, and as I suspected he wanted no part of highsounding words, but a simple explanation of why his prayer style should change. So I went on to say that change was not being made for its own sake, but to provide a concerted effort to bring human custom into line with our personal relationship with God. For so long we've used the priest as our link with God. Of course there was personal and private conversation with God through prayer, but the Mass was primarily the priest's act, and except for our physical presence, we had little part in the action.

Then I sprung this bit of theology on Dad. As human individuals we are also members of a holy people, an assembly, when we gather in church. As such we make, as we participate with the priest and our neighbors in the Mass, an individual response which is also communal, and we do that in a tongue we understand, Latin for some, and one's own language in the case of most.

Some actions are proper to the priest while others are shared, for example, the singing, the music, answering the responses, praying the intercessions, etc. The Constitution on the Liturgy emphasizes that, "if those prayers and actions of the liturgy no longer speak to men so as to teach them, this meaningless activity is to be replaced."

Dad chided me a bit about the "meaningless activity" thing and wryly indicated: "You mean my going to Mass all these years was meaningless?" I ducked that one and went on to tell him that music, costume, and even rhythmic dance proper to a people will be part of the Mass of the future. I told him how different were my confirmations in the black parishes of our archdiocese as compared to the more stead practices of the white parishes. He remembered that I had written something about the black archbishop from Africa who celebrated Mass during the Council in gaily-colored vestments and to the accompaniment of drums.

The constitution on the liturgy is clear that while change is the keynote, what is essential is change of heart. And that again gets back to the basic trust of Pope John's Council, the inner renewal of ourselves and the Church.

January 11, 1964

To put the question that ended my letter to you last week: Are we really interested in expressing the "aggiornamento," that change of heart that Vatican II is looking for? And if we are interested, are we ready for some good listening and study? Let's not get bogged down with the conquest of the material – so many things to do, so little time for quiet discernment of the "why" of the changes in our Church.

The document on the liturgy will soon become part of our implementation in our parish. In your everyday world, in your formal and informal meetings, in your conversations, your listening, your outlook, how will you reflect your Church, what with all that the media is saying about her. The way we pray and worship is now the most obvious change – other things will follow: How we celebrate the sacrament of baptism, the new look at the rite of reconciliation, confirmation, marriage, the anointing of the sick. Will you be ready to take part in this new age of renewal, an age we hope and pray will be the brightest in modern church history.

I'm hinting at the meetings and conferences your parish priests are planning, come Lent, to implement the new liturgical directives.

Come to learn about the seven chapters that comprise

the constitution on the sacred liturgy: The general rules; the chapters on the Eucharist, the other sacraments and sacramentals, the divine office or the liturgy of the hours which the priest prays every day; the liturgical year, the "why" of Sunday, the feast days of the year, and the special place our Blessed Mother Mary has in the liturgy; sacred music, and sacred art and furnishings. It's a fascinating array of subjects that should make our Lent more than just the usual fasting, weekday Mass attendance and the other devotions proper to that time of the Church year.

You will learn that certain portions of the Liturgy document will need to be legislated by our National Conference of Bishops in order to take effect. The Constitution that specifically states that, "no other person, not even a priest, may add, remove, or change anything in the liturgy on his own authority." And you will learn that certain changes will require our bishops to ask Rome for permission.

Understandably, the revision of liturgical books, the missal we use at Mass, the composition of new rites, will require several years of scholarly work before they can be acted upon. A special commission is in charge of this. So come and hear what we can and cannot do about changes in the liturgy.

An obvious change will be the absence of the prayers of the priest at the foot of the altar. In its place will be a greeting and a short penitential rite. Another change, readings will be done by other than the priest, except the gospel, unless there is a deacon or another priest present. The priest will be expected to give a homily at every Mass at which people are present. It used to be called a sermon. From now on, the readings of the scriptures for the day will be emphasized and explained by the priest.

There will be a formal presentation of the "gifts" for the celebration of the Mass – the water, the wine, and the hosts to be used at that Mass will be brought up to the altar by members of the congregation. And, it might be that the usual collection will be taken up before the priest proceeds with the Offertory prayers.

The basket containing your contributions will be placed at the foot of the altar and, in a symbolic manner, offered up with the gifts of wine and water and the hosts. The words of the Constitution state: "It is desirable that the participation of the faithful be expressed by members of the congregation bringing up the bread and wine for the celebration of the Eucharist or other gifts for the needs of the Church and the poor."

Just prior to communion, the priest will invite us to exchange a symbolic "kiss of peace," probably a handshake with the person or persons next to us. Our Lenten meetings will explain in some detail the reason from that, as well as the new rite of receiving communion under "both species," that is, the host and a sip of the Precious Blood.

And finally, you will notice that the priest and his attendant ministers will be processing into the Church from the rear, as well as processing out at the end of Mass to the accompaniment of song. The Entrance Song, as it will be called, is to foster a "deepening of the unity of the people." I like to think that as the priest moves down the aisle toward the altar, singing along with the people, he is embracing the whole assembly of people and inviting it to join him in the celebration that is about to begin. Perhaps too, he is showing that he is coming out from among the people to take his place in the sanctuary, to lead the community in prayer.

Now and then, on certain feast days or even Sundays if more than one priest is present, they will concelebrate the Mass together. The old custom of the priest celebrating the Eucharist at a "side altar," or in some chapel privately will be discouraged. The Constitution is quite insistent that "liturgical functions are in no sense private functions but celebrations of the Church which is the sacrament of unity that is the sign of God's oneness and the undivided character of his love for us."

And while I'm quoting the Constitution, here is more that may be of interest to you: "Each person, minister or layperson, who has an office to perform, should do all, but only, those parts which pertain to his or her private office by nature of the rite and the principles of the liturgy." Lectors, commentators, and members of the choir are specifically mentioned in this context. The priest has his role and the other ministers of the Mass have their roles. For instance, only the priest may pray the Canon of the Mass; only a priest or a deacon may read the gospel and preach the homily.

So there is a quick glimpse of the liturgical changes of the future. I would urge you to get acquainted with these changes, their reasons, so that you can participate intelligently in the Mass of the future.

January 18, 1964

We are on the brink of a new era of familiarity with the Bible by virtue of the Constitution on the Liturgy. The Bishops of the Council set an example for that in the many ways that the Sacred Scriptures are quoted in the Council documents.

The Constitution itself states that, "there is to be more reading from the holy scripture, and it is to be more varied and suitable . . . preaching should draw its content mainly from scriptural and liturgical sources . . . Bible services should be encouraged, especially on the vigils of important feasts, on some weekdays in Advent and Lent, and on Sundays . . . the treasures of the Bible are to be opened up more lavishly, so that richer fare may be provided for the faithful at the table of God's word."

What will happen is that instead of the two readings we now have there will be three. I suspect that publishers will be coming out with special lectionaries that contain those readings for Sundays and the holydays of the year.

Then as to the rites themselves, the Council Fathers urged that they be marked by a "noble simplicity, short, clear and unencumbered by useless repetitions; within the people's comprehension."

The color of vestments and the whole liturgy of funerals will be changed to emphasize the paschal character of death as it was done in ages past. Couples will be encouraged to get married at Mass; the sacrament of Confirmation will be administered during Mass, as will the sacrament of Baptism.

January 25, 1964

In my last letter to you I mentioned that much of what we bishops accomplished, at least in the area of the public worship of the Church and the more extended use of the Bible, would have been impossible without the help of the liturgical and biblical movements that preceded the calling of the Council of Vatican II. That also holds true of the many "periti" of experts that assisted us in Rome.

In a sense, those periti dominated the first session of the Council and understandably so. A good number of them were called to Rome by Pope John to assist in the preparatory phases of Vatican II and the early position papers presented us were obviously prepared by them. However, as the bishops got "their feet wet" and adjusted themselves to the workings of the Council, they took over and began, especially in the second session, to express their own views. This is not to indicate that the periti had no further role in Council proceedings. Contrarily, they continued to assist the bishops and were sometimes called upon, in study sessions and in the preparation of interventions, to provide their expertise in certain areas.

Our Cardinal, a biblical scholar in his own right, often called upon two experts in scripture studies to assist him in the preparation of interventions he would be making before the Council. Then again, certain bishops brought with them private specialists of their own choice whose status was different from that of the official periti of the council, the kinds Pope John called to Rome. These specialists would assist their bishops in areas in which they intended to participate in Council discussions.

Father John Courtney Murray, for instance, a Jesuit priest and an American, was brought to Rome as a consultant by Cardinal Spellman of New York. Father Murray achieved acceptance for his expertise in the area of political and religious freedom. He will be an invaluable guide to us in the next session of the Council when a document on Religious Freedom comes up for discussion.

Now, some of those periti, and Father Murray is just one example, may be unfamiliar to you, but believe me, he and his colleagues will become household names in the future, as their contributions become more publicly acknowledged. They played a key role in the Council proceedings, and that was all to the good; after all, they brought to the Council floor the fruits of years of scholarship and special study.

Many of those periti shouldered the tiresome burden of drafting, revising, and correcting the texts of the documents submitted to them by the Secretariat of the Council. When it came time to present a final draft of a much debated document, some bishop got the credit.

Understandably, it was a Council of the Church to which bishops were invited and who alone could vote. The theologians knew that and quietly acknowledged that the conciliar committees were their field of work. But there was more to it than that.

For some of us bishops another vital arena of theologian-bishop relationship was not St. Peter's Basilica where prelates gathered for discussion and debate, but some quiet room in one of many of Rome's colleges or seminaries. There, very often, of an evening, sometimes after a good

111

Italian dinner, we took off our shoes, disregarded our collars, and exchanged learning and experience.

Sometimes, it was the living room of a pension where bishops and periti resided. Bishop O'Donnell and I often frequented such a pension on the Piazza Hungaria where several of our American experts lived and to which they would invite their counterparts from other countries. Of an evening those present might be Father Murray, Father Hans Kung of Germany, or one of my favorite theologians, Father Karl Rahner. We picked each other's brains and learned much of the behind the scenes work that was going on in committees.

Then again, we received announcements of lectures that were being presented by the periti at particular colleges on subjects germaine to our discussions in the Council. I recall a pleasant evening at Rome's college for German seminarians where Father Karl Rahner spoke. He is considered to be the most exciting and profound theologian of our time. Pope John appointed him to that prestigious group of periti who are the official Council theologians. He also serves as consultant to two Cardinals, Koening of Vienna and Doepfner of Munich, who were frequent guests of Cardinal Meyer at our Chicago House of Studies.

One particular evening, at the German Seminary, Father Rahner regaled us with his vision of a Church renewing itself and a Church of the future. With thought-prodding questions he felt that each generation must rethink the problems of theology for itself. He did not, of course, reject the theological decisions of past councils or Popes, but asked what those decisions of pronouncements mean in our day.

An example: In the Council we've been working on a document on the Nature of the Church and who makes up membership in the Church. With regard to the Pope and the bishops, Father Rahner felt that the highest authority in Catholicism is not the Pope, but the Pope in union with his bishops. The term collegiality is used here, or more specifically, the College of Bishops with the Pope. So that, when the Pope speaks on something affecting the whole Church, he does so as the head of the College of Bishops who collectively are the successors of the Apostles.

As for the Church of the future, Father Rahner has a fascinating view: "A World Church, a Church no longer Western-European but a Church in which the third world countries will play a vital part in its renewal."

January 31, 1964

This will be my last letter to you for awhile. Mixed in with a bit of vacation, I will be attending meetings in Palm Beach, Florida, of the new Bishops' Committee for Ecumenical Affairs to which I have been appointed. I'll have to tell you more about how that came about later. Then there will be a gathering of Diocesan Directors of the Liturgy in Dallas, Texas in the middle of February, and a meeting of the Administrative Board of Bishops in Washington toward the end of the month.

March 15, 1964

During the next weeks, my reports on Vatican II will be sporadic. After all, as your pastor I do need to focus on the needs of our parish.

Meanwhile, here is more of our Vatican II work on the subject of Ecumenism to which I only briefly referred in my past letters to you. Pope John XXIII, in calling us to Rome for the Council, did emphasize Christian unity as being at the heart of his dream for this twenty-first Ecumenical Council of the universal Church. He put it this way: "Ecumenical councils, whenever they are assembled, are a solemn celebration of Christ and His Church and hence lead to the universal radiation of truth . . . in the present order of things, Divine Providence is leading us to a new order of human relations – the unity of the Christian and human family.

In outlining the agenda for the Council the Pope went so far as to express the hope that, "those who, though claiming the name of Christian, are yet separated from this Apostolic See, may listen to the voice of the Divine Shepherd and approach the one Church."

The most dynamic expression of the Pope's dream and desires for Christian unity was exemplified in the presence of forty Protestant Observers at our Council meetings. Day after day, five to six times a week, these observers witnessed the intensity and spirituality of daily Mass. They were exposed to the warm hospitality of the bishops, rubbed shoulders with them and dialogued with them in the "coffee bars."

It must be emphasized that the observers were not there simply to sit and observe. Their opinion on a wide variety of matters was sought and discussion was promoted on key issues through the Secretariat for Christian Unity. Then again, it seemed that every time the Holy Father attended our meetings he made a special effort to recognize the members of the other churches.

Two issues particularly interested the American observers, several of whom I knew from my work with Catholic Relief Services and our common efforts for the victims of the last war. One was the statement on religious liberty which we would be trying to finalize in the next session as well as a proposed statement on the Jews.

Religious liberty is part of the American scene which produced the separation of Church and State, and it is in that context that both the Catholic and Protestant churches flourished so well in our country.

As for the Jewish statement, large numbers of Christians in our country and elsewhere, have been concerned with the problem of anti-semitism. The statement we are studying acknowledges that certain tendencies and teachings in Christianity have caused an unjust persecution of the Jews. Witness the holocaust of the last war as it sought to eliminate the Jewish race entirely.

Those two issues are not, of course, the central issues of the unity which the Council of Vatican II seeks. Their importance cannot be denied but there is a wider aspect to the unity which we seek in the Council.

Of perhaps greater importance are the substantive issues that divide Christianity: The power and role of the Pope, as well as that of the bishops in their day-to-day administration and activity in their local dioceses; the belief in the real Presence of our Lord in the Eucharist; questions involving ministry, the validity of sacred orders, the number of sacraments, and the role of the Blessed Virgin Mary in the economy of salvation.

March 29, 1964

On the matter of our relationship with our Protestant coreligionists about which I wrote to you in my last letter, there is more you will want to know. Last January, our Cardinal Archbishop addressed a group of Protestant ministers and provided not only leadership but further enlightenment in that area of the unity which we seek among our churches.

Speaking to those ministers at the Chicago Theological Seminary, Cardinal Meyer emphasized that there is much that unites our churches in a pastoral way. He spoke of a special letter he was sending to the priests and people of the archdiocese on the subject of ecumenism with its practical implications from the standpoint of the theological virtues of faith, hope and charity.

In the mind of the Cardinal, "Ecumenism is an attitude of mind and heart that must express itself in action. It consists of our really listening to Christ's prayer for unity, and to His promise that this unity is really possible." You do, no doubt, remember our Lord's prayer at the Last Supper to which the Cardinal was referring.

"The unity of Christians," according to Cardinal Meyer, is "indeed impossible from a human point of view, but in the light of faith we know that it is a goal made possible through the power of the Spirit. We need to have hope in this power."

In going on to explain the nature of the unity we are talking about in the sessions of the Second Vatican Council, the Cardinal emphasized that it is not just any kind of unity that we seek, but the very unity Christ prayed for – a visible union, yet not a mere natural unity of a single organization produced by human organizing ability, like a corporate merger, or a political alliance.

It is also something more than a unity of brotherhood and friendliness, even more than "a genuine Christian love and hope for mutual salvation. "What is sought," the Cardinal felt, "is a genuine unity of faith, since only on this firm foundation can charity and hope really abide in permanence." He even felt that this unity of faith is compatible with the diversity that characterizes our churches.

What I think the Cardinal had in mind was a statement made by Pope Paul VI at the opening of our second session of Vatican II last September. The Pope stated that: "This mysterious and visible unity can be realized only in the one faith, in partaking of the same sacraments, and by a suitable link with a single supreme leadership of the Church, even though different languages, rites, ancient traditions, local privileges, ecclesiastical currents, legitimate institutions and freely chosen particular ways may be permitted." I believe that it is this latter sentence of the Pope that the Cardinal had in mind when he spoke of "compatibility despite our differences."

We do need to keep in mind that an important ingredient of unity is faith, and true faith, moreover, as the

Cardinal puts it is "not simply a vague trust in God, but an acceptance of definite truths." What that means is that in our ecumenical dialogue, unity cannot be achieved by any compromise in matters of faith. Somewhere I heard or read that in our relationships with other churches we need to search out ever more honestly what we have in common rather than what divides us.

April 1, 1964

At a meeting the other evening a number of our parishioners commented how much they enjoyed my letter on ecumenism. Here is more on that subject and I build on the very last sentence of the letter of March 29 which says: "In our relationships with other churches we need to search out ever more honestly what we have in common rather than what divides us."

During our Council sessions many bishops emphasized that we, as teachers, have a continuing responsibility to have you, the laity, understand the distinction between what is of faith, and therefore unchanging, and what is merely of Church law or Church practice which can be changed.

For quite some time, I was personally involved in ecumenical matters for the Church. In the area of social concerns, and in the alleviating of the consequences of World War II. I worked closely with our Protestant and Jewish brethren in bringing relief and rehabilitation to the victims of that war. In another area, I represented, and continue to do so, our American bishops on several theological-dialogue teams: the Angelican/Roman Catholic dialogue; as chairman of the team that met with the Disciples of Christ and as vice-chairman of the Roman Catholic/Jewish team. One of the most hopeful signs of that experience is that almost all of the leaders of those denominations agree that unity cannot be achieved by any compromise in matters of faith.

In other words, unity cannot be bought at the price of any form of religious indifferentism and nothing would be gained by any compromise with truth. Truth is an absolute that cannot be diminished.

But the perspectives from which we view truth and the angles from which we approach it are continually changing. Thus we grow in knowledge of the truth. What is necessary, as I see ecumenical dialogue these days, is understanding of the position of the other side and to have our own Catholic side understood by them. From such understanding we can discover how our own positions and theirs have suffered from long centuries of controversy.

From such understanding, I have discovered how our own Catholic theology must be purified and expanded through richer and deeper insights that are made known to us. That thought reminds me of Pope John's exhortation to us bishops at the opening of Vatican II when he urged us to "open the windows, let in some fresh air, and wipe away the dust from long centuries of controversy."

My fervent prayer is that we learn more and more to drop our own prejudices and gain understanding (even when we must continue to disagree), so that our separated brothers will grasp even better the religious kernel of our convictions and see our Catholic faith in what we consider its true light.

So it is, my dear friends, that we have entered into a new stage of inter-faith relationships even though as American Catholics, we hold firmly to the belief that ours is the one true Church. After all we must try to live side by side with other denominations in a pluralistic society that is typical of our country.

And I'm not saying that one religion is as good as another but that we cannot exploit effectively American religious resources, unless all religions work together for that ideal which the Founding Fathers of our country had in mind.

I'll have more to say about that in my letters from Rome next Fall when we tackle the Council document of Religious Liberty.

The next time I write to you I'll try to provide some examples of ways in which we can work together.

May 2, 1964

When I wrote to you last month about some examples that might illustrate the cooperation that could enhance the goal for unity among our Christian Churches, I had in mind something of the following – things that underlie the religious-socio-political tensions that exist between us.

For example, in the field of morals, there is the question of birth control and the question of the place of religion in education and the related problem of state-aid for parochial schools. These seem to hold the first place. In the theological arena we differ, of course, with the celebration of the Mass and the Real Presence of Christ in the Eucharist, and our veneration of the Blessed Virgin Mary.

But underlying all those tensions is the number one question for Americans of all religious persuasions, that of religious liberty. We'll not solve many of our differences until the subject of religious liberty is further developed. At the Council next fall we bishops are looking forward to that development as already contained in Pope John's encyclical, "Pacem in Terris," or "Peace on Earth," in which he said: "Every human being has the right to honor God according to the dictates of an upright conscience and the right to profess his religion privately and publicly."

In the fifth chapter of the document on Ecumenism which we approached last year, religious liberty is considered, but we put off serious discussion of that subject to another time. The issue really has deep interest for us American bishops and we would like to see developed a separate document by the Council on that subject.

In looking forward to its discussion in the next session, we know that the text can be perfected and we will have to seek the cooperation of the so-called Catholic countries of Western Europe who, as yet, don't see the importance of religious liberty. Some bishops, especially from Italy and Spain, take the position that religious freedom is a threat to the faith of many Catholics, especially those less educated. A bishop from Spain insisted that religious freedom would allow the Protestants to proselytize Catholics in Catholic countries.

Just talking to some of my bishop friends from behind the Iron Curtain last year about the subject of religious liberty reminded me of these words of Father John Courtney Murray, an expert on this matter: "For centuries the Church has been looking in on herself, but if and when this subject of religious liberty does come up, as it must, there will be need of the Church's experience in America and of the wisdom that has been at the root of this experience as it must now be applied to the countries who are denied religious freedom."

As I indicated earlier, the basic thrust for discussion of the Religious Liberty text is present in the Council's document on Ecumenism, that is, that every person who follows his or her conscience in religious matters has a natural right to true and authentic Religious Liberty.

Cardinal Meyer, in that talk to which I referred to last month, did insist that: "The Church does not admit that any man is free to obey or disregard God's will as he chooses." And in reference to the Council's text on Religious Liberty, he pointed out that the document itself does say that, "a man can do God's will only as he knows it."

Thus, even though a person's conscience be in error, if it is a sincere conscience, formed after earnest effort to find the truth, it represents God's will to that person and that person must follow it. Perhaps that's getting a bit too deep for you to understand this matter of Religious Liberty. So, simply put, Religious Liberty affirms a basic principle: a person's duty to worship God, and a natural right to freely express that faith.

But then, there's another step we need to take when we talk about ecumenical dialogue. It has to do with the related question of conversion. Conversion must always be the result of a person's earnest effort to find the truth and to form one's conscience in accordance with this finding. That's why I do not see why there needs to be any opposition between the dialogue which aims primarily at understanding, and the continuing mission of the Church "to preach the Gospel to every creature."

The purpose of dialogue with our Protestant friends is not, therefore, to win arguments, but to achieve understanding. The work of conversion is, after all, the result of God's grace.

June 5, 1964

Vatican II will forever be remembered as Pope John's Council and there is much that could be said about the objectives he had in mind for that Council. Among those objectives was his strong plea for unity among Christians. "Here is the reason for our joy which surpasses the first thoughts we had when preparations were made for this world gathering: 'Deign, O Lord, to grant peace and unity to a united Christian people.'"

But beyond that, his addresses revealed the position he desired his bishops to take: neither the condemnation of heresy, nor even the assertion that doctrine is the principle concern of the Council. More than anything else, he wished the Council to show that the Church is the vital and energizing center of society. He wished the Church to be understood in its maternal aspect of embracing all men and women.

Pope John stressed two points of his ecumenical spirit:

First, there was official encouragement to an attitude which recognizes openly and publicly that the responsibility for disunity must be shared by all, ourselves included. He did that in these words: "We do not wish to put anyone in history on trial; we shall not seek to establish who was right and who was wrong. Responsibility is divided. We only want to say: Let us come together, let us make an end of our divisions."

Second, in calling the Council, the Pope made it clear that the great contribution of the Church to the common quest for Christian unity is to seek her own reform: "The revival of Christian standards of morality, and the bringing of ecclesiastical discipline into closer accord with the needs and conditions of our times. This itself will provide an outstanding example of truth, unity and love. May those who are separated from this Apostolic See, beholding this manifestation of unity, derive the inspiration to seek out the unity which Christ Jesus prayed for so ardently from his heavenly Father."

July 10, 1964

Do you remember your catechism definition of the Church – One, Holy, Catholic, and Apostolic? Let's look at that definition in the light of my recent letters on ecumenism.

Do you know that there are other churches who believe that they are also, One, Holy, Catholic, and Apostolic? Let me explain. In the Vatican II document on the Church which we bishops hope to see finished and promulgated by the Holy Father in the next session, there is this sentence: "This Church, constituted and organized as a society in the present world, subsists in the Catholic Church, which is governed by the successor of Peter and by the bishops in communion with him. Nevertheless, many elements of sanctification and truth are found outside its visible confines. Since these are gifts belonging to the Church of Christ, they are forces impelling towards Catholic unity."

That sentence would imply that the Church of Christ is not solely identified with what we know as the Roman Catholic Church. There could be, and it seems there are, other Christian churches that may be identified because of their beliefs as a Church of Christ. Of course, we're different and I'll try to spell out those differences by explaining those words of the creed we recite: "One, Holy, Catholic, and Apostolic."

Unity, our oneness, is best exemplified in the fact that the Mass, the sacrament of the Eucharist, is celebrated everywhere in the same way. True, since Vatican II, we use different languages, but it's the same Mass that transcends language, culture, and nationality. The document on the liturgy does provide for adaptation to the needs of the local faith communities, the color of vestments, for instance, music accompaniment and the like, but in essentials the Mass is our Eucharist no matter where we are. There's a beautiful sentence in the document on the Church to which I referred to earlier: "Each individual part of the Church contributes through its special gifts to the good of the other parts and of the whole Church."

I need not tell you how many Protestant churches there are, each a part of the Church of Christ, but celebrating their faith and liturgies in different ways.

There is an abiding holiness in the Catholic Church despite the sinfulness of its members and here the word grace is important. Our Protestant friends believe that they are holy by virtue of their faith in Jesus Christ. In contrast we hold that faith and good works are necessary, that the power of grace which comes to us through the sacraments and those good works makes us acceptable to God. Remember, in the Creed, we express our communion with the saints, honor them and pray to them so that they may

123

be an example to us of holiness.

Our Catholicity is very closely related to our unity. We are part of every race and culture and we reach out to all levels of human existence. Our Catholicity is enriched by the fact that grace builds on nature, that our faith and the way we reason out our faith is deeply rooted in holy scripture and tradition, in sacrament and above all in the Cross which is our glory and the victory Christ won for us.

Protestants feel that we've complicated our religion. That our faith is too juridical. Some say that we're a hodge-podge of different practices; the cult of Mary, all those devotions, that being Catholic means we have to bring in the Pope, the sacraments and a lot of other things to please all kinds of people.

Apostolicity is where we are divided with Protestantism in a "Grand Canyon" of differences. Protestants believe that apostolicity hinges on the Bible alone. Our view is that is not enough. We believe that our Lord put Peter at the head of the Church and that bishops are the successors of the apostles, and as a result, that there has and always will be a continuity in sacraments and ministry, and more than that, a living authority in the Church.

Protestants, on the other hand, again feel that we complicate things by bringing a hierarchical church between the faithful and God, that we're too preoccupied with ritual, dogma and law, that we leave little room for the working of the Spirit in our lives.

Vatican II did a lot to clear up that false impression by emphasizing, in the Dogmatic Constitution on the Church we'll be considering next fall, that the Church, as institution, is not an end in itself, but that it consists of a People of God, laity and clergy, working together in holiness, for advancement of the Kingdom of God on earth.

August 1, 1964

Last month I was invited to Loyola University by Father John McKenzie S.J., the scripture scholar, to share with faculty and some of the summer students an informal discussion of Vatican II. Since our local media had emphasized the impact Cardinal Meyer was having on the Council, the group was particularly interested in the nature of his interventions and a kind of update of Council proceedings. Next month your bishops will be leaving for the third session of the Council so perhaps a summary of that meeting at the University may also be of interest to you.

Pope John XXIII is, if I may use the word, the hero of Vatican II. After all, it was no achievement to have launched the Catholic Church into a new era of its history. The reform and renewal of the most ancient and continuous institution of Western civilization was not a simple matter to initiate. It took courage for the Pope to call the bishops to Rome and tell them that, "each believer is a citizen of the world and that we need to bring the modern world into contact with the gospel, and to do that we need to read and understand the signs of the times."

Some of those signs on the horizon in the early sixties were, for instance, Holy Scripture and Catholic reform of the way the sacred writings are interpreted; the renewal and fostering of the liturgy, and the quest for unity among Chnstians. Our very first work, and the very first document to be promulgated, that on the Liturgy, put Pope John's vision this way:

"To intensify the daily growth of Catholics in Christian living: to make more responsive to the requirements of our times those Church observances which are open to adaptation; to nurture whatever can contribute to the unity of all who believe in Christ; and to summon all of mankind into her embrace."

Of course there were those bishops in the Council who

reacted to that and stood up to say: "Beware of contagion with the world. I understood them because I remembered that in my seminary days I was allowed visits from my parents twice a year, no visits home, even for Christmas or Easter; no magazines or newspapers; women were evil!

Yet, in an early and more positive intervention of a document that would come under debate in the third session of the Council, our Cardinal said, "This document appears to fear contagion of the world too much. I think this is because of an insufficient emphasis on the theology of salvation and the bonds which redemption has established between God and man. Our work in the temporal order is part of the transformation which God plans for the world."

I'll never forget an expression which Pope John used in his book, *The Diary of a Soul*, "We must infect the world Christ."

The Third Session
of Vatican Council II

September 14, 1964 - November 20, 1964

September 10, 1964

I started to write this letter on the plane as we were returning to Rome for the opening of the third session of Vatican II but because of rain in New York we got a late start. By the time dinner was served around ten-thirty that evening I was too tired, and what with a glass of wine for dinner, I dozed off.

Before long, in the Eastern horizon I noticed the sun rising over the coast of Ireland. Soon after, and as the stewardess was offering us breakfast, we were over France. Then came the exciting scenery of the snow-covered Alps. The captain told us that within the hour we would be skirting the Italian coast line in the vicinity of Genoa - and beginning our descent into Rome's Fumicino Airport.

As our huge plane began its lowering circle over the Adriatic toward the airport there were again out of the little window the sight of ancient walls, an old aqueduct and the kind of beige-brown and cream coloring of farmhouses that dotted the landscape.

Need I tell you again how much I love Rome, its narrow streets, its shrines and churches, old familiar places, the galleries and of course the sight of St. Peter's Dome in the distance.

Soon, within the week, we'll be under that venerable dome poring over the documents that will shape a new look for our Church. Indeed, "Roma aeterna," eternal

Rome, as the phrase has it, changing with the times but still surrounded by the traditions of an ancient culture and faith. So, with our church so old yet so ever knew and ready we bishops hope to read and adapt to the "signs of the times."

At dinner this evening, despite a bit of jet lag, here at our Chicago House of Studies, we were trying to answer the question, "What is the state of the Council?" We agreed that the first session might be described by the word "groping." The second session, one in which we gained experience and made ready for conclusions we hope to adopt in this third session that will begin next Monday.

One of the students here, from his studies of Vatican I, recalled the experience of Pope Pius IX, who presided at that Council and who is to have said that there are three stages to a Council: "That of the devil who seeks to destroy everything; that of men who put everything into confusion, and the third stage in which the Holy Spirit puts all things in order."

Some at the table agreed those same stages might be applicable to Vatican II. Our Cardinal proposed a more studied view. He agreed that the first session had its disturbing moments and that we were, given our inexperience with the working of a Council, much too eager to take advantage of the liberty Pope John had given us. Most bishops were, according to him, unfamiliar with the preparatory phases of the Council, and very many were unfamiliar with the "way things are done in Rome and in the church."

He used the Italian word, "Patienza," to describe the attitude we might adopt. I feel he said that because we younger bishops, and especially those of us who had pastoral experience, were inclined toward quick and radical changes. I feel also that our speedy adoption of the liturgical movement and the rapid adaptation of those changes in the liturgy over the past year spoiled us.

September 18, 1964

Last Sunday, the 14th, Pope Paul VI formally opened the third session of the Second Vatican Council with a concelebrated Mass. Twenty-four prelates surrounded him at the main altar of St. Peter's. Two American archbishops were among those, Shehan of Baltimore and Krol of Philadelphia. Pope Paul VI apparently did this to emphasize two points in the talk he had at the end of the Mass where he said that he was not only the head of the apostolic college of bishops but their brother and that together the bishops were the "teachers, sanctifiers and rulers of the Christian people."

The Pope went on to remind us that the central task in the third session was to complete the first Vatican Council's teaching on the Nature of the Church by explaining the role and function of the bishops as successors of the apostles. He surprised many when he expressly welcomed, "our beloved daughters in Christ, these first women in history to participate in a conciliar assembly."

Thirteen proposed documents face us in this session. We were advised that six will be open for discussion and seven will merely be presented as "propositions." I have a feeling, just from listening to some of my brother bishops here, that the bishops will generate discussion on those so called propositions from the floor because of their importance. I know that our Cardinal intends to speak to and raise to another level the proposition on priests. The other proposals include, missions, the Oriental Church, the role of religious men and women, seminaries, Catholic schools, and marriage.

The six "key" schemas include the one on the Church to which the Pope referred in his opening talk to us: the schema on the controversial discussion on Religious Liberty, a section on Jews and non-Christian religions; the important schema on Revelation that was tabled soon after the first session of Council started; a schema on the Lay

Apostolate, and what has become the famous "schema 13," on the Church in the Modern World.

We faced much of the material in those documents last year but it appears that the commissions charged with reducing the number of subjects (more than seventy when the Council was first called), and more importantly, obliged to consider the many interventions made on those documents in the past, have come up with much improved and more inclusive schemas for our consideration.

There is some skull-duggery here that "schema 13," on the Church in the Modern World, because of its conformity to Pope John's beautiful encyclical, "Pacem in Terris," will receive star billing in this session. However, I believe that the schema on the Nature of the Church and the one on Revelation will also rank at the top. In any case, given their approval and promulgation sometime in the future, those three documents will have, I feel, a great impact on the way our faith is practiced in the next century or more.

A Protestant observer whom I knew from the days of our war relief efforts in the 40's mentioned that the problem of mixed marriages would need to be considered as a test of how far the Church is willing to go to establish a good ecumenical atmosphere.

And there appears to be some change in the offing as far as procedures are concerned. Cardinals, like the rest of us bishops will have to submit their interventions in writing five days before they ask to speak; the number of speeches will be curtailed and the moderators or chairpersons will urge bishops to speak on behalf of a number of their confreres – for instance, one bishop representing the whole of the hierarchy of one country or region.

As I moved about St. Peter's after the opening ceremony I renewed old friendships with bishops with whom I sat in the section of those tiers that comprised our desks and places. There are a few more bishops from behind the Iron Curtain.

At dinner the other evening we talked about the concelebrated Mass and Pope Paul's desire to see to the proper implementation of the Liturgy document, our first completed work of the Council. We wondered whether the more conservative bishops would again retard the progress so many others were hoping for. The Pope apparently wants to get things moving. The Italian press reported that he had spoken to the Italian hierarchy about their conservatism and lack of understanding about the world outside Italy.

Cardinal Meyer made note of the fact (as he judged the Pope's talk at the opening ceremony last Sunday) that the Holy Father considered this third session a crucial one and that we would be in for some surprises. Well, there was the first, the presence of women representatives. At our first meeting on Monday, not really a working session, the Pope observed that, "these measures (the inclusion of women in Council deliberations) were taken so that women will know how much the Church honors them in their human dignity and in their Christian and human mission."

September 21, 1964

The eightieth general meeting, the first of the third session, began last Tuesday, the 15th and we got off to a fast start . We wound up the debate of the seventh chapter of the schema on the nature of the Church that had to do with "the last things," such as death, resurrection, immortality and judgment. There was no mention of hell, so one of the Cardinals, Ruffini, Cardinal Meyer's friend from Palermo, insisted that some mention of hell should be included because of those who die in the state of mortal sin.

Another bishop felt that too little was said about Purgatory. All in all, fourteen Council Fathers spoke that morning and since there were no others asking for the floor, the Moderator called for an end to the debate. We were back at the Chicago House by one o'clock for an earlier lunch.

Our discussions about those "last things" were frequently interrupted by bishops who spoke about the role and place of the Blessed Virgin in the schema on the Church. Some were for a whole special document on the Virgin Mary, others favored, and I think this will win out, that a former schema on the Blessed Virgin may be incorporated as a separate chapter in that schema. Most of us accepted the thinking of those bishops who said that "after all, Mary was, as we all are, among the People of God."

In essence, that special chapter would explain Mary's role as it is described in Scripture and handed down through the ages in Tradition; her cooperation with Christ in the work of salvation and the application of those truths in teaching and preaching.

But here again, our debate on the role of the Blessed Virgin Mary was interrupted by several Council Fathers who brought up the matter of the canonization of saints.

Let me explain their interruptions: The bishops hand in their names requesting a place on the agenda, then because of the large number of speakers, they may not be called upon for lack of time. But present their views they must. And so, the Moderator not having seen the speaker's text, calls upon him and the speaker begins to address a subject we had considered a day or two before or even in the past. Sometimes the Moderator would urge the speaker to speak to the matter at hand, but in charity allows the man to go on with what he wanted to say but was not given the opportunity.

Know that the case of the canonization of saints we were involved in, came up during the last session when we were discussing the People of God, that universal call to holiness and the fact that we are a pilgrim Church striving for heaven.

Cardinal Suenens of Belgium started things when he

said that the Church aims at producing saints but that the process may be questioned. He felt that a large percent of the saints are members of the clergy who belonged to religious orders, that at least ninety percent of those belong to countries like Italy, France and Spain, and that the investigations for sainthood are prolonged and extremely expensive. He felt that sainthood should include persons from all nations, classes and callings.

A bit of humor was introduced when the Archbishop of Westminster in England rose to complain about the accumulation of those "dry bones" mostly from Italy. So you see, we had our light moments too. But seriously, there was a great deal of talk about leaving those investigations on sainthood in the hands of the local bishop as it was done in the Middle Ages.

September 26, 1964

I'm getting ahead of myself because there is so much to report to you about the exciting things that are going on here in Rome. Voting began on that important document on the nature of the Church. 2,289 bishops cast ballots on the first chapter of that schema and the secretary advised us that we would continue to vote on subsequent chapters of the document with the hope that the entire schema might be approved and promulgated in this third session of the Council.

At our meeting on the 17th, a good deal of time was spent discussing the title to chapter eight, the last chapter of schema on the Church, concerning the Blessed Virgin Mary and her role in the economy of salvation. Back and forth we went with titles like, "Mary, Mother of the Church," "Mary, Mother of all Believers," or "Mary, Mother of God." In the end sentiment seemed to turn to the latter title which has a long tradition in the Church and good foundation in the Sacred Scriptures.

On Friday last, the 19th, the interesting, and what I feel will be an innovative concept of who make up the Church of Christ on earth, chapter two, on "The People of God," was voted upon by 2,190 bishops present.

That concept of "The People of God" provided interesting discussion about who constitute such a people, in reality, who are the members of the Church. An archbishop from France put it well when he said that, "both the pastors (bishops and priests) and the laity belong to the people of God and that the hierarchy springs from the faithful as a means of achieving the Church's purpose.

Some basic wording of the text as we voted on the concept goes like this: "At all times and in every race, anyone who fears God and does what is right has been acceptable to Him . . . He has willed to make men holy and save them not as individuals without any bond or link between them, but rather to make into one whole those who acknowledge Him and serve Him in holiness . . . the one People of God."

On Wednesday, the 23rd, we began the rather controversial discussion on Religious Liberty. Three of our American Cardinals were among the first to speak to the subject. A year ago we received the first draft of a proposed "Declaration on Religious Liberty." Then you may recall, I mentioned that such a declaration was part of the document on Ecumenism. As a matter of fact the proposed declaration was drafted by the Secretariat for Promoting Christian Unity. I consider our discussion of this subject of such importance that I plan to write you a special letter that should follow this one in a day or two.

September 30, 1964

Well, today we had an interesting morning. We embarked on some discussion of a declaration on Jews and non-Christians; then the early chapters of the schema on Divine Revelation were introduced. I'll get to these matters, but in keeping with my promise, here is more on the subject of Religious Liberty.

Three of our American Cardinals spoke out strongly in support of the proposed declaration on Religious Liberty. They were Cardinals Cushing of Boston, Ritter of St. Louis and our own Cardinal Meyer. The latter announced that he was speaking in the name of practically all the American bishops who attended a recent meeting we had to discuss the declaration.

In his address, Cardinal Meyer emphasized that the document on Religious Liberty was in accord with Pope John's encyclical, "Pacem in Terris" (Peace on Earth). He gave five reasons why the declaration was necessary in our day: one, that all men expect from the Church religious liberty; two, because it is necessary for the Church to give an example on how governments should treat religious bodies in their countries; three, that true religion consists in the free, generous and conscious acceptance of God; four, that the church in its evangelization mission give the example that no one should be led to the Faith by force; and five, that its declaration could lead to fruitful dialogue with other religions. In the conclusion of his speech, His Eminence went so far as to say that if the declaration is not passed, nothing else enacted by the Council will make much difference.

Cardinal Cushing emphasized the point that the declaration was much awaited by non-Catholics and summed up his speech by saying that its contents exhibited a "decent respect for the opinions of mankind." Cardinal Ritter was not as sanguine about the text we had before us. He introduced the subtle argument that there be two votes on the document when it come to that stage: one on the acceptability of its substance and the second on the reasoning supporting it.

Oh, by the way, I did tell you that during the past summer months we had much to do in responding to the draft of the documents that would be coming up in this third session of the Council. It was interesting to learn from Bishop DeSmet of Belgium, who introduced the declaration on Religious Liberty, that 380 observations were sent in on this document alone and that all had been carefully considered.

Cardinal Ruffini, our old friend from Palermo, Italy, was the first to speak on the Religious Liberty declaration and he proposed what many felt was quite an orthodox approach. He felt first that the title should be changed to "Freedom to Profess Religion," or "The Free Exercise of Religion," and that we should not confuse freedom with tolerance.

"Freedom is proper to truth," he said, and "only truth has rights." Well, that had a lot of the bishops buzzing. And then we came to attention when a bishop from Spain declared that he wanted a complete revision of the document. His objection surfaced the feeling that existed in many so called Catholic countries where Catholicism was the dominant faith. He conceded that while the declaration favors union with those separated from our faith it also ignores the grave dangers to the faith. The bishop felt that the declaration was written for "Protestant countries."

I was happy to hear the intervention of Cardinal Silva of Santiago, Chile whom I knew and with whom I worked to establish Catholic Relief programs in Chile in the 1950's. The Cardinal, familiar with the inroads of proselytism by various sects in his country had the courage to say that the declaration would have special impact on the work of evangelization in Latin America. He stated that his people needed "a new Christianization and that this document would be a step to purer apostolic activity and not stop at simple proselytism."

The last speaker of the day was a bishop from behind the Iron Curtain and I, for one, was anxious to have someone of the Fathers living under Communism say something on this document. A Bishop Cekada from Yugoslavia directed the declaration's content to where it really belonged. He noted that Communism always strikes at Religious Liberty when it is in position to do so. He asked that the "Council Fathers send an appeal to the United Nations to issue a declaration proclaiming the obligation of certain governments to respect religious liberty and all forms of religious activity."

As you might guess, between the 23rd of September and this writing there was a veritable barrage of pros and cons on the Religious Liberty document. In addition to the initial debate I have just outlined, there is, I feel, the need for you to know a bit more about other developments relative to the freedom to practice religion.

The Austrian Cardinal Koenig of Vienna, a good friend of our Cardinal and a frequent dinner guest at our home here, added weight to the intervention of the Yugoslav bishop I mentioned earlier. The Cardinal begged all of us present not to forget the "tragic fact" that many nations under Communism are deprived of religious freedom and their leadership is militantly atheistic.

There were also, in the past few days, more than two dozen speakers who objected to the draft on Religious Liberty in its present form. The very essence of our problem was that we were trying to work out a theological concept of religious liberty, for something which many of us were unprepared.

A highly respected American theologian, Father John Courtney Murray, at a press conference, provided a bit of that theology when he said, "It is a large step from freedom with which Christ has made us free; (Gal.5/1) and the technical sense of freedom. The Council is preoccupied with linking the former with political structures and the whole problem of civil liberty." He gave the United States as an example where, as he put it,

> "The free exercise of religion is governed by the order of society – that is public order. This is made of three civil goods: one, public peace; two, public morality, including the notion of public health; three, harmony in the exercise of civil rights. Religious liberty is subject to the same norms."

You will hear more from me on this subject when we get to the actual vote on the document. It will be interesting to see how the "powers that be" here in Rome handle that subject of Religious Liberty in which we Americans are so vitally interested.

October 3, 1964

I do need to report to you on how we came out with that statement on our relations with Jews and non-Christians. On the 28th, strong support for a positive statement of the Church's relation with Jews was supported by four of our American cardinals. Our own Cardinal Meyer, although supporting a broader concept against discrimination of any kind on the grounds of race, color or creed, asked for consideration of the text we had received last year. He felt that the original document was more ecumenical and that it was not enough for the Church to deplore any kinds of injustice against the Jews, but that we ought to point out the close relationship of the Jews with the Church.

Cardinal Meyer was further supported by his friend Cardinal Ritter of St. Louis who also urged the restoration of the original text. But he went further. He emphasized that it is often wrongly assumed that God abandoned the Jews and the Jews were rightly to be accused of the condemnation of Christ. Cardinal Meyer pointed out to us later that St. Thomas Aquinas, the great medieval theologian, taught that the Jews were not formally guilty of deicide.

And I should mention that there were some strong objections to having any statement on the Jews come out of the Council. Having lived for several years in the Middle East, I could understand the feeling of several of the patriarchs of that area who felt that the declaration on the Jews could cause trouble for Catholics because of the hostility of the Arab world to such a statement.

Cardinal Tappouni of the ancient city of Antioch felt that although he was not opposed to Judaism as a religion or to the Jews as a people, a statement from the Council on the Jews would be promoting political ends rather than religious ones. I've a suspicion that he is right and I tried to argue that point with our Cardinal. Having witnessed the division of the Holy Land between Arabs and Jews in 1947, I feared for the future of the Church and its people in the Near East.

The two-day debate on the Church's relation with the Jewish people ended in a compromise. Rather than a separate and specific document on the Jews, the direction seems to be that a more comprehensive statement will come forth about the Church's relation with all non-Christian religions.

October 6, 1964

We're moving along, as you can tell from the way my letters to you follow one upon the other. There is so much to write about that weekly or even bi-weekly letters would not cover all that is happening in the Council of Vatican II. Perhaps you've noticed that lately I have not reported too much of the social side of our lives here in Rome. Oh, there have been a few dinners and interesting guests at our home here, and there was one "vijaggio," or small trip into the country if one could call it that.

Bishop Grellinger, the auxiliary bishop of Green Bay, Wisconsin and a close friend of Cardinal Meyer, suggested a "bus trip to the end of the line" the other day.

What we did is select a bus line that originated here in Rome and traveled the longest distance into the suburbs. After two hours of stops and goes, we terminated around lunch time in a little community about twenty miles from Rome. We sought out the usual and typical sidewalk cafe. First we had an aperitif of "Cinzano" on ice, a brand of vermouth we use in cocktails at home. Then the waitress-cook, a rather portly and extremely friendly person, told us there were just two things she could prepare for us, a pasta with clam sauce or veal. We decided on the pasta.

After about a half hour there was placed in front of us a huge plate of spaghetti with clams in their shells, and to our surprise two pieces of veal on the side. The waitress, who turned out to be the wife of the owner and the chief cook, explained that since we might be the only customers that day there was no point in saving the veal for tomorrow. Needless to say we were cajoled to provide a handsome tip.

It was dinner time by the time we returned to Rome and after settling for a bowl of soup we repaired to our rooms for more study of the documents that would face us on the morrow. We would begin debate on the schema on Divine Revelation – the interpretation of Sacred Scriptures and the place of Tradition vis-a-vis those sacred writings. To put it another way, whether everything contained in the tradition of the Church is found in some way in the Bible or whether oral tradition extends beyond Scripture and contains things not to be found in it.

There will be therefore, few decisions we will be making in this Council that are more delicate and fraught with consequences for the Christian life of believers than those pertaining to the nature of revelation and the sources of Christian doctrine or teaching. Pray for us that the Spirit of Truth guide us in our deliberations.

You will recall that the document on Divine Revelation was given to us in the first days of the opening of the Second Vatican Council in 1962. But such was the controversy over the schema that the Pope decided to shelve the draft document and appointed a special commission to prepare a new schema. That is how it happened that Liturgy became the first document we debated on instead of the Revelation and the Sources of our Faith.

At long last, therefore, after two years of work, the schema on Divine Revelation was brought to our attention on Wednesday, the 30th. We were presented with a majority and a minority report of the 24-member Theological Commission that worked on the schema. The crux of the problem centered on the relationship between the Sacred Writings and Tradition that I explained to you earlier in this letter.

As was expected, Cardinal Meyer, a scripture scholar, highly respected and eagerly listened to by the Council Fathers, took the floor.

The Cardinal sided with the majority view of the special commission that worked on the new schema on Revelation. Key to this view was his feeling that Tradition is broader in scope than the Bible and that it is not always free of human defects. He also alluded to another point of controversy, that of how the Sacred Writings are to be interpreted today, that is, with the use of modern scripture research and methods, which he favored.

The history of that controversy goes back to Pope Pius XII who had written his encyclical "Divino Afflante Spiritu" in 1943 promoting biblical studies and research in a more modern way. In our early sessions of the Council in 1962, the opposing forces to that encyclical came forward again and added another reason why Pope John directed the schema to be rewritten.

Cardinal Meyer gave the following examples of how the living tradition of the Church deviated from the ideal and is not, therefore, always free of human defects. He cited the exaggerated moralism of the past centuries, private pious practices which have eaten away the real spirit of the liturgy, and the neglect of the Bible, and even the active discouragement of Bible reading by Catholics.

I should tell you that our Cardinal's good friend from Palermo, Italy, Cardinal Ruffni, another scripture scholar who studied in Rome with Meyer, supported the minority view. What a session we had at dinner one night this past week when the two of them voiced their opposite feelings about the schema on Revelation. We had a preview of what was going to happen in St. Peter's in the week ahead of us.

Sure enough, as my English neighbor at the Council said, there'll be a circus with this schema on Revelation, on just how God's word of salvation was handed down to us through the centuries. Twenty bishops took to the floor last Thursday to speak.

If I may, here is a brief summary of what part, probably the most controversial, this schema on Revelation is all about. It will help you understand the various viewpoints as I allude to them later on. First, a definition:

Revelation is the opening of God to man in a plan of salvation that consists of action and words. In the Old Testament that intervention of God in man's history can be understood as an encounter between two persons: one person speaking and the other listening. Recall how God spoke to the prophets and they endeavored to fulfill His wishes for the people they represented.

In the New Testament, revelation took a different approach. As the letter to the Hebrews put it: "God, who at the sundry times and in divers manners spoke in times past to the fathers by the prophets, last of all in these days has spoken to us by His Son" (1/1).

Salvation was promised us after Adam and Eve had sinned (cf. Gen 3/15) and God's purpose and means becomes clearer through Abraham, Moses and others in the Old Testament, and ultimately through Christ in the New Testament.

Tradition is defined as the "total being and the action of the Church, in its life, in its doctrine, and in its worship, whereby the mystery of salvation is implicit and passed on through the ages." It's not that there is added new content to what is in scripture and tradition, but a better or more progressive understanding of the mystery of salvation under the constant influence of the Holy Spirit. Our basic dilemma in the Council, therefore, was resolution of the question: are there two separate sources or just one source of Revelation?

Now I feel that's about enough for you to digest in this reading. More on these exciting days in my next letter.

October 9, 1964

What lessons we bishops are getting these days in Scripture. It reminds me of my seminary days when we were taught how to interpret the Sacred Writings from the original Hebrew and Greek texts. But this problem with tradition is, if I may use a popular word, really "bugging us."

It all comes down to how some of us here understand the word "tradition." Some Council Fathers restrict the use of the word to "apostolic tradition," that is, to the period in which the apostles lived, and they claim that it is wrong to speak of tradition as living and always evolving. Cardinal Meyer, and I believe the greater majority of us here, use the word tradition in a broader sense to include not only the apostolic period but the development of doctrine as the Church moves through history. We feel that God, through the Holy Spirit is always providing us with direction toward our salvation.

Let me remind you that the present teaching of the Church is that not all the doctrines of our faith are in the Bible. That teaching is the crux of our difference with our Protestant friends who believe that Sacred Scripture is the unique and self-sufficient source of the rule of faith.

Today, we ended our debate on the schema on Revelation. Let me summarize what we finally ended up with.

One, determination not to open up again debate of the problem of the two sources of Revelation that caused so much disagreement in our first session in 1962, and as a matter of history, in other Councils that preceded this one.

Two, whether there is one source or two, is not so important as affirming that Scripture and Tradition together transmit to us the one Gospel preached by the apostles. One and the other subsist in each other, if I can put it that way. After all, the Bible itself is written tradition.

October 15, 1964

I should tell you that not all was debate since we came to Rome a month ago. In between all that discussion I've been describing to you, we voted on certain sections of documents that were completed. For instance we agreed to streamline the voting on the schema on the Nature of the Church and as a result most of the chapters (we voted separately on these, as well as on certain amendments to those chapters) were passed.

On October 5th, we plunged into the beginning of the fourteen votes that would decide the fate of the three chapters that comprised the document on Ecumenism. On the 6th, we ended debate on Revelation and began discussion of the new schema on the Role of the Laity in the Church which emphasizes that lay persons are not only in the church but that they are Church. We were advised that certain laity would be addressing the Council on that document.

In between, we received reports of the votes on the ecumenism document which passed overwhelmingly. On the same day we learned that a document on the Priesthood would be introduced within a week or so and that some specially chosen priests were invited to participate in our discussions.

Cardinal Ritter of St. Louis started off the debate on the text of the document on the Laity. He called for a redrafting of the schema on the grounds that, as it stands, it is too clerical and patronizing in tone, and too juridical in the sense of its non-pastoral relationship between laity and the hierarchy. And rightly so, he called for a theological basis for the lay apostolate that was so beautifully expressed in chapter four of the schema on the Nature of the Church.

A number of other prelates voiced similar feelings but I feel that the gist of the speeches centered on what I suspect will be quite an extended role for participation of the laity in the mission of the Church.

The document itself speaks of the Apostolic Vocation of the Laity in that as members of the Church they cooperate, in their own manner in the mission of the Church which is to continue the work of Christ on earth. This call or vocation is the lay person's right and duty flowing from union with Christ in the sacraments, particularly the sacrament of Baptism.

As for the different fields of activities in which the laity would cooperate with their bishops and priests, the schema mentions the family and the church institutions such as the diocese, the parish and even the Church universal. The family as such radiates an apostolate through example. As for the diocese and parish, the talents of the laity need to be brought to use not only in the government of those institutions but in the expansion of their spiritual purposes.

One of the American prelates from the West, Bishop Leven, not only expressed happiness that at long last the role of the laity has come before the Council, but emphasized strongly that real dialogue between bishops, priests and the laity is needed. Participation of the laity in the work of the Church is not simply a concession but their right. Again, I am reminded of the strong phraseology that was written into the document on the Church in that regard and to which I alluded earlier. The present schema has this challenging sentence: "the Christian impregnation of the temporal order achieves the goal of creation, which must be in its entirety recapitulated in Christ for the glory of God."

145

Another American, Bishop Ernest Primeau, a classmate of mine, drew applause with his remark that "the day has ended when the role of the laity in the Church was simply that of pray, pay, and obey."

Archbishop McCann of Capetown, South Africa made the interesting observation that lay persons are often more talented and better trained for certain fields of work in the Church than priests. He foresaw laity doing not only clerical and so-called housekeeping tasks in diocesan and parish offices, but taking on administrative roles as well. Several speakers last Monday, however, emphasized that laypersons be provided with some type of spiritual formation as well as understanding of the Church's mission. I'm thinking now of how our Catholic schools are doing just that.

On Tuesday, a layman, Mr. Patrick Keegan of England, was chosen by the lay auditors at the Council to speak for them to the schema on the Lay Apostolate. On the same day we learned that four American pastors were invited to attend the rest of this session of the Council along with priests from other countries, presumably in preparation for our discussions on the Priesthood document.

Mr. Keegan expressed the hope that our schema on the Lay Apostolate would be the beginning of a whole "new stage of development" in the role of the laity in the Church and he offered "loyal cooperation in fulfilling the noble aims of the document."

Yesterday, Wednesday, we began the much anticipated discussion of the document on the Priesthood. I noticed our Cardinal typing away in his study what I suspect will be a critique of that schema because on the way home from that day's meeting he told us how much he disliked the short shrift priests were getting in our Council discussions.

October 20, 1964

Sure enough, when discussions began on the Life and Ministry of Priests, there was acknowledgment that priests are the forgotten ones of the Council. They have been, so far, placed between bishops who got a lot of attention in two documents, the Constitution on the Church and the Decree on their Pastoral Role in the Church, and the Laity, who will be spreading their wings and influence.

There was real effort over the past few days to change that viewpoint. At Pope Paul's personal request pastors from various parts of the world were asked to sit in on our discussions. There priests mingled with us in the coffee bars and did not hesitate to make suggestions to those bishops who would be speaking.

Originally scheduled as a full blown schema, the present document on priests has been reduced to that of a set of 12 propositions, one of the least important forms for a document that normally are not scheduled for debate. Cardinal Meyer was the first to speak out and was listened to with reverence followed by applause when he said: "I must reject this draft as unacceptable. I urge a full schema and full discussion of the subject, just as there had been for bishops and the laity. The text speaks only of obligations without a word of comfort and encouragement of priests. This does not serve the good of the Church."

Discussion of the text ranged over a wide area, from priests' salaries, medical care, retirement benefits, their spiritual lives, etc. The bishop from Lourdes in France decried the fact that too many of the faithful look upon the priest as a mere functionary. The laity need priests and they are closer to them than we are, he said.

Several bishops proposed the establishment of advisory councils of priests to aid bishops in their administration of the diocese as also associations of priests which encourage their updating of the Church doctrine and the like; others thought that the relationship between pastors and their assistants could be improved. One bishop felt that stole fees, that is charges for administering the sacraments, should be abolished. Another deplored the tendency of priests to put aside their clerical clothing, that the cassock has been disregarded.

A crucial observation by a bishop from Spain involved the future relationship between priests and laity when the latter become more prominent in Church mission and administration. The bishop felt that some form of special training be provided in that area of shared responsibility. I thought that was well put. Priests could be very jealous of their position.

Then came the startling observation of an Archbishop from Brazil who said "The text of these propositions is poorly done, they're an insult to the priesthood. There is too much haste here, the text should be entirely re-written and brought back to us in the next session of the Council." The Archbishop's intervention was greeted with general applause. And then when the Secretary of the Council, after some twenty bishops had been heard, announced that voting on the propositions would be delayed to a later date there was more applause.

October 22, 1964

Well, we did some voting since the last time I wrote to you. On the 19th, the Council Fathers gave overwhelming approval to the seventh chapter of the schema on the Nature of the Church and that our destination is heaven. And, as we say in Latin, "mirabile dictu," (wonder to behold), we voted to send the propositions on the priesthood back to the commission for complete revision.

And there was this milestone; we began discussion on the long-awaited text of schema 13, the Church's Relationship to the Modern World. The document is the brainchild of Cardinal Suenens of Belgium and of Pope Paul VI. The first speakers included eight cardinals, they always had preference; among them, Cardinal Meyer who rose to say that, "he was unhappy with the impression given by the text that the Church fears contagion from the world."

He called for a better understanding of the role of the world in the whole plan of God's salvation. He cited scripture and tradition and St. Paul's teaching on the economy of salvation which involves not only salvation of souls, but the resurrection of bodies and transformation of the universe to which bodies belong. He called for "a compenetration between the world and the Church," and observed that work here on earth pertains not only to the temporal order but to the everlasting as well. "By his labors," the Cardinal said, man "prepares for the final transformation of all things into a new heaven and a new earth." The talk was greeted with enthusiastic applause.

It was quite a technical intervention, if I may put it that way, but what His Eminence wanted to get across was that, we, through our various vocations in the world can transform it according to God's plan; by our activity in every field of endeavor we can contribute in a positive way to the fulfillment of the divine plan. After all, this is our world, the world we have helped to make and in which we must find our living and salvation.

It was a heady day and I needed a walk. After lunch and a short nap I directed my steps toward the inner city. As you move about Rome, "Roma eterna," as they say here, you can't help but recall the Rome of the past, the Rome of Caesar and Cicero, and contrast the old with the new. Only remnants of ancient villas remain surrounded by modern apartment buildings. The new Rome seems to have served notice on the old that it will devour it in the name of democracy and progress. The old monuments, their statues, carvings; the columns of the ancient Forum of Rome, even the Coliseum show the deterioration of a polluted atmosphere. They're even beginning to cover those reminders of the past with plastic seeking in a fruitless effort to preserve them.

Where Puccini, Liszt, Verdi, Keats, Shelley and many of the classicists walked and meditated among the oaks and pines on the music and poetry that enriched our lives, today the radio blares out the latest strident rhythms for the delight of young Italy astride their noisy Vespas (gasoline powered cycles).

But that is not the whole story either. Where only a few had enough to eat and the means to enjoy something of life, there are now many. Where only the few could read and write and learn from art their history and faith, the Rome of today, like so many other cities over the world, is far more literate, far more intent upon increasing its power over matter.

As I think about Cardinal Meyer's intervention on a schema that will look to the new in terms of the old, to a relationship of the Church to the world, I feel, maybe as he does, that something has been gained but something has been lost. We still have wars and rumors of others to come; we still have poverty and we've done so much to despoil God's creation.

In addressing itself to the world in and of our times the Council has under consideration in schema 13 another outstanding document. Whatever will be its fate after it has undergone the usual scrutiny of the bishops here and felt the whiplash of their criticisms, it deserves to be seen as truly magisterial in its scope and amplitude.

Many of us here feel that schema 13 is the brave new world of all of our aspirations, the world of hoped for equality and justice, of peace, of genuine religious liberty and political freedom; about man in and of the modern world. The document strives to set forth in unmistakable terms what the Church thinks of man, about his greatness and his misery, and how, as the Cardinal intimated, he should set about securing some measure of his temporal redemption as a reflection, here below, of his eternal salvation.

The schema on the Church and the World, schema 13, is long, maybe too long for popular reading, maybe even too theoretical and philosophical, but it tries to approach the ideal. If the words Cardinal Meyer spoke at its initial presentation have been heard, it can never be said henceforth that the Church is afraid to speak to the modern world, that it is not only concerned with itself.

October 27, 1964

It seems pretty definite that I'll be back here next year for the fourth session of Vatican II. Bishop John Wright of Pittsburgh, who serves on the commission that drew up the document on the Church and her Relationship to the World, schema 13, told a group of us the other day that "debate on the schema will take many weeks and that we may not finish that debate on the schema during this session of the Council."

That exciting schema because of my sociological background I will find very interesting. There is consideration of the Church and man's calling; the dignity of the human person; the community of mankind; man's activity throughout the world; the role of the Church in this modern world; the nobility of family and marriage; the proper development of culture; economic and social life; life of the political community; the fostering of peace in the world chapters.

Chapter One deals with our vocation as Christians living in the world. Added to those chapters and sections are five very long appendices which cover a good number of practical and specific problems that deal with our living in this world with an eye to that salvation promised us by the Lord.

There is consideration for the dignity of marriage and the family in the world today; the sacred character of marriage; conjugal love; the fecundity of marriage. Another appendix considers the cultural situation in the world today, the direction of the natural and human sciences, sometimes to the detriment of what one might call the "humanities;" economic and social life, political life, that whole area of the peace we seek on earth.

As I said earlier, it's quite a document this schema 13 and I can understand why it's going to take us a long time to debate its contents.

By the way, we learned today that the draft document on the Role of Laity in the Church, after some 64 speeches by the bishops, went back to its commission for revision. We were also told that this session of the Council would end on November 21st, and that the fourth session will begin whenever the Pope decides. The Secretary, Archbishop Felici, expressed the hope that several of the documents now pending might be finished, approved and promulgated at the end of this session. We'll see!

"The switches are now thrown in the right direction" said Cardinal Koenig of Austria at a press conference the other day. He felt that expectations in regard to schema 13 were a bit high and that the document cannot provide a cure-all for all the world's problems. He did feel, and I think most bishops here go along with him, that the document "can lay down general principles and give some indication of the directions the Church might pursue in dealing with contemporary world problems."

This morning, debate started off on how poverty afflicts, almost as a plague, so many parts of the world, the principle theme being a more equitable distribution of the world's goods. One astute observation made by a bishop from a poor country seemed directed to us in the United States. The bishop noted that while God's perfection consists in what He is, man's perfection stems from what he has. He observed that this "having" can easily run riot and pervade a person's whole being.

For the second time, a Catholic layman addressed the Council. James Norris, one of my associates in Catholic Relief Services, described the specter of hunger-ridden poverty that breeds disease and despair and finds relief only in death with such conviction that he was applauded long and hard. He quoted a passage from Pope Paul's last Christmas message which said, "We must make our own the sufferings of the poor. And we hope that this sympathy of ours may enkindle a new love which, through a specially planned economy, will multiply the bread needed to feed the world."

Cardinal Suenens, the inspiration behind schema 13, brought up the situation of women in the Church. He insisted that the "Church must abandon its masculine superiority complex which ignores the spiritual power of women." Last year the Cardinal accused the Church of neglecting "half of humanity" and this morning emphasized that "we must learn to respect woman in her true dignity and appreciate her part in the plan of God." Although recognizing that the presence of the women auditors in the Council was a step in the right direction, Suenens insisted that once this Council is over they must continue to have an impact on the life and work of the Church.

A bishop from Germany echoed this position, "The Church has not yet become aware of the world-wide implications of the changed position of women in modern society. Women should be accepted as the Church's grown-up daughters, not just children. In the liturgy they should be addressed directly as 'sisters' and not just submerged in the salute 'brother.'

The terrible problem of racism was brought up by my good friend, Archbishop Patrick O'Boyle of Washington, with whom I was associated for many years in Catholic Relief Services. The Archbishop has a very large population of black people in our nation's capital. He called for a "forthright and unequivocal condemnation of racism in all its forms."

Needless to say many bishops, especially from the third world countries, rose to support and expand Archbishop O'Boyle's appeal to rid the world of racism. Bishops from Africa spoke of how racism continues to enslave especially women. But one of them made a remark that could be applied to all women, namely:

"Women must be brought to a full acknowledgment of their own responsibility. Woman is not just a servant, a handmaid, a mother or and instrument of pleasure, but man's helpmate and companion."

October 31, 1964

The other day we plunged into the long-awaited subject of marriage and birth control. The coffee bars were virtually deserted as the bishops remained at their desks to listen and speak on a subject that was of virtual pastoral concern to them. Applause greeted many of the speeches, the most enthusiastic I've heard so far.

Archbishop Dearden of Detroit, a member of the Theological Commission that worked on the document on the Church in the Modern World, presented the report on family life. He struck a discordant note in the beginning when he announced that the Pope had reserved to himself the particular question of the use of birth control pills and the naming of a special commission he would set up to study the question.

"The document, as drafted by the commission, "said Archbishop Dearden," lays down the principle that fecundity in marriage should be both generous and conscious." By this he meant that judgment about how many children a couple should have belongs to the partners in that marriage; however, their decision should be made with a correctly formed conscience and according to the mind of the

Church. As for the use of the pill, the Archbishop felt that was such an intricate matter "discussion on the floor of the Council would be unable to settle it."

Then came the fireworks. Cardinal Ruffini of Palermo Italy, as usual, led off the debate. He maintained that the text leaves the door open to all sorts of abuses by leaving the final judgment on this important issue of procreation to the individual. Cardinal Suenens, on the other hand, urged the Council to be courageous in facing up to pastoral demands and called "for an objective study of the theology of marriage on the grounds that the traditional outlook has been too one-sided." He then said that "all facets of the problems need to be explored and that modern science may well have to tell us about the use of the pill."

Cardinal Leger of Montreal, Canada was applauded when he said, in support of Suenen's position, that "some people fear any revision of the theology of marriage and that many of our difficulties in this field stem from inadequate explanations in theological manuals concerning the purposes of marriage."

The 'pieced d' resitance' came when the Patriarch of Antioch rose to say, "we shepherds gathered in council need to have the courage to approach squarely present-day problems in marriage out of love of God and love of souls." If I may put the almost fifteen minute speech of the Patriarch which was enthusiastically applauded, in capsule form, he said; "There is a question of a break between the official teaching of the Church and the contrary practice of the vast majority of married couples. The very authority of the Church is called into question."

"Frankly," continued the Patriarch, "the official position of the Church on this matter should be revised on the basis of modern theological, medical, psychological and sociological science. I wonder whether the official position might not derive from a bachelor psychosis on the part of persons unfamiliar with marriage."

November 7, 1964

We had a four day holiday because of the feast of All Saints and All Souls and it was an interesting weekend. Rome can get a bit "stuffy" with the air pollution that comes from thousands of vehicles spewing carbon dioxide into the atmosphere. You know, we have four rush hours here; one in the morning and another in the early afternoon, a third in late afternoon and the fourth in the evening. Italians work through the morning and return home for lunch. Then, after their siesta, they return to work into the evening hours. And that makes for the movement of a lot of traffic.

So it was that in the interest of breathing in some fresh air, Cardinal Meyer suggested a trip out of town; two trips as a matter of fact. Last Sunday after Mass we took off for Bracciano, a quaint town in the hills north of Rome and famous for its great and deep lake that supplies some of the "virgin" drinking water for Rome. After an hour's walk about town, we found an interesting outdoor cafe overlooking Lake Bracciano.

What a lunch we had; first, a salad of mixed vegetables, then the usual pasta dish, and after that, the most tender slices of veal I ever ate. Oh yes, there was the customary bottle of local wine, and it was good. Dessert was a kind of pudding with a caramel sauce. We returned to Rome by early evening for a very, very light supper and more Council homework.

On Monday, after we celebrated the Masses for All Souls Day, the Cardinal suggested a trip to the famous Benedictine Monastery at Monte Cassino founded by St. Benedict in 579, and time permitting, a visit with the famous stigmatist Padre Pio in Foggia whom he knew. Cassino is in a mountainous area some 60 or so miles southeast of Rome and Foggia another 55 miles further to the east near the Adriatic Sea.

The famous landmark monastery at Cassino was destroyed by aerial bombardment during the last war because the Allied commanders wrongly believed that it was occupied by German soldiers. The abandoned ruins however, were later taken over by the Germans. Thousands of Polish soldiers attached to the British fifth army lost their lives there in the effort to dislodge those German forces who used the ruins as a strategic overlook of the valley below. We spent almost an hour moving about the cemetery below the monastery where those soldiers are buried.

After the war, the Italian government rebuilt the monastery where we had lunch and a tour of the new building. Cardinal Meyer was anxious to learn if any of the ancient manuscripts and books were saved. We learned that what books had survived in the lower regions of the abbey were sent for repair to Rome and Germany. So warm was the hospitality of the monks and, therefore, so protracted our stay at Cassino, and what with a rather heavy rain beginning, we decided to forego the trip to Foggia and leave that for another holiday.

Our 114th meeting, by the way, began on the 4th, with a discussion about the possibility of a special Synod of Bishops that would assist the Pope in the governance of the Church. The idea came out of a discussion we had on a document I have not mentioned to you before, that of the Pastoral Office of Bishops, that is, their duties and responsibilities as shepherds of the Church. The concept of such a so-called senate of bishops was voted on by an overwhelming majority of the bishops. You must remember that this idea of a special group of bishops helping the Pope through periodic meetings with him was a logical step in that discussion we had on the Church as a People of God sharing in the responsibility for the whole mission of the Church – collegiality was the phrase we used.

The bishop who gave the report on the particular chapter that referred to a special advisory group to meet with and advise the Pope, kind of watered down the idea of shared responsibility when he said that "a central commission of bishops meeting with the Pope should not be regarded as a representative body of bishops, but rather as a symbolic sign of the Council Fathers' desire to cooperate with the Pope." After that, my neighbor from England passed a piece of paper over to me with a large question-mark on it.

Yesterday Pope Paul VI broke an age-old tradition by deciding to preside over a working session of an Ecumenical Council. It was an indication that he wanted to demonstrate his interest and exert his influence on the Council's draft document on mission work which was coming up for discussion.

The Mass yesterday was unusual and many of us wondered what might have been going through the Holy Father's mind when he heard his bishops clapping to the beat of tom-tom drums. The Mass, sung in the Ethiopian Rite and a native language called "Geez," was an example of how the liturgy of Vatican II could be adapted to the local culture of peoples. One of the black assisting priests wore a "tintinnabulary headgear carrying small bells," according to my well informed and much traveled English neighbor.

In his brief address, the Pope said: "After undergoing some final changes, I hope the text before you will be easily approved by you and what pleases me most is the constant emphasis throughout the document that the entire Church should be missionary."

One of the Church's leading scripture scholars, Cardinal Bea, who is also the head of the Secretariat for Christian Unity, reiterated the Holy Father's viewpoint that, "missionary activity is part of the Church's very nature."

One of the principle criticisms of that text on the missions was that since last January when we bishops had received the document for study and comment, the draft had, on orders from the Coordinating Commission, been reduced to 13 propositions.

I should tell you that the Coordinating Commission, which was brought into being by Pope John at the end of the first session of the Council, had acquired in addition to supervising the works of the Council, the unhappy task of seeing to the shortening of the sometimes voluminous documents before us, and above all the reduction of their number. You might recall that we started out with some 73 documents. As of today just 2 have been promulgated by the Pope and 14 more schemas await final votes and approval. Given the present pace of our work here, some of us feel that we'll be coming to Rome for the next five years or so.

November 11, 1964

More on the mission work of the Church. Cardinal Agagianian, the head of the Congregation in Rome for the Propagation of the Faith, provided us with some interesting statistics. He pointed out that in 1870 there was not a single native bishop in the Church's mission territories. Today there are 167, including four cardinals. Within the last fifteen years the number of Catholics subject to his office rose from 28 to 50 million.

Naturally then, the chief criticism of the draft text on the missions centered on the fact that the document had been reduced to a mere 13 propositions from an original schema of seven chapters. A bishop from India introduced a bit of humor relative to that reduction when he said that, "mountains are in labor but are producing merely a mouse."

Most of the speeches we heard in the past few days were given by bishops living and working in the mission areas of the world. One of those, an Irishman from Rhodesia in Africa, made a hit and was applauded for his criticism of the document before us. This Bishop Lamont said: "We expected not bare, simple propositions, but meat, and not dry bones. I would hate to think that the glorious missionary work of the Church is to be reduced to a few naked proposals." The good bishop then asked if any of us were inspired to sacrifice new effort for the missions, "If this schema has not moved us to greater effort, how can we expect to inspire the heads of our religious orders and their members who are the prime movers in the field of spreading Christ's message of salvation?"

And then again Bishop Lamont's Irish humor prevailed when he said that our missionaries are asking for "modern weapons and we're supplying them with bows and arrows. Here in Council we asked for bread, but it seems we're getting some stones called propositions, let's put flesh, and nerves on the bones of this schema, breathe life into it."

At the end of the meeting the Secretary for the Council announced, in an atmosphere of disappointment, that debate on the missionary text would end on the 9th and that we would need to proceed to further discussion of schema 13.

Monday, the 9th will be a day to remember. Six speakers took the floor on the subject of missions, among them our own Bishop Fulton Sheen. Applause interrupted his interventions time and again. There was a kind of exhilaration the meeting inspired, I think, by one of the bishops who said that the whole document on the missions should be sent back to the writers for complete revision. This, despite the fact that the Pope had made a personal intervention on the text and "hoped for its acceptance with some revisions."

Of course, you could hear a pin drop when Bishop Sheen rose to address the Council on the subject of the missions. As head of the Propagation of the Faith Office for the United States which annually provides between ten and fifteen million dollars for the missions, the bishop was a familiar name and figure to most of the Council Fathers.

After suggesting that the definition of mission be broadened to include not only those in pagan or non-Christian countries but those among us who were still "unchurched," Bishop Sheen plunged, as only he could, into an impassioned plea for the work of the missions. He said: "I am a servant of the missions and I would like you to know that during all these three sessions of the Council many bishops who are living in great poverty come to my seat in the Council Hall. They come from territories where there are only seven or ten priests to care for 50,000 square miles."

"I ask," said Bishop Sheen," is it Christian, is it Catholic, and is it worthy of the charity of Christ, for me to say to those bishops, I cannot help you. How far does that doctrine of collegiality we discussed so much extend?"

After waiting for the applause to die down, Bishop Sheen ended with this observation: "Poverty stalks the mission world. Put your finger on the 30th Parallel, run it around the globe of the earth, lifting it slightly above China, what do you find?"

"Practically all the prosperity is above the 30th Parallel, and the greater part of the poverty of the world is beneath that Parallel, that is Africa, Asia, and Latin America. As only a wounded Christ could convert a doubting Thomas, so only a Church wounded by poverty can convert a doubting world."

With Bishop Sheen's ringing plea for the missions still in our ears, we returned to work yesterday to face a discussion on the status of Religious Life. Recall that, the mission text was remanded to its writers for revision. We'll hear about its fate later.

November 14, 1964

There are many bishops in the Council who are members of religious orders. I'm anxious to hear their reactions to the text of the document on Religious Life after they learn that its content was reduced from 100 pages to 30 and now to just five pages!

Bishop Joseph McShea of Allentown, Pennsylvania introduced his commission's report on the document on Religious with an apology for its brevity. He stated that strict orders from above, probably the Coordinating Commission, brought that about. Much of the contents of the schema on religious, an introduction and 19 propositions, are of a technical nature that may be of little interest to the layperson.

However, you may be interested in proposition 12 that states, "the religious habit should be simple, modest, poor, yet becoming, hygienic, up-to-date and practical. Habits which, in the Holy See's judgment, do not conform to these standards, will be changed." Or there's the first proposition that says, "The spiritual and religious renovation of every religious institute and their adaptation to modern requirements are to be pursued under the Church's guidance."

Cardinal Spellman of New York, the only American to speak yesterday, took a cautionary stance regarding the modernization of religious life this way: "The work of modernization and adaptation should proceed under proper guidance but nothing should be done under the plea of aggiornamento (renewal) which empties the religious life of its purpose and significance. Nothing must be suggested and nothing must be done in the name of modernization which would prevent Religious from bearing their essential witness to Christ by their vows, by their life, by their life of detachment from the world and the things of the world."

We learned that there are some two million religious in

the world of whom one million, two hundred are women. The other day seventeen bishops spoke to the text of the document on Religious, among them the heads of the three largest communities of men. It's apparent to you, I presume, that at present, women religious have no voice in what we men will say about their religious lives.

At a press conference after our meeting, Sister Mary Luke, an American auditor at the Council, expressed what I feel were the sentiments of many Sisters, when she said that religious women would like to have "some representation in the bodies which govern their lives."

After eight speakers had expressed their views, a vote was called for on the Propositions on Religious. The Propositions were passed by a narrow majority of votes with the proviso that they be sent back to the proper commission and a final vote later on. A final note was struck by one of the bishops who said that the text of the document on Religious was "incurable," and that the writers of the text should elicit the help of the Sisters who are Council auditors in its revision.

On the 12th, after those votes on Religious Life and with little time left that morning, we proceeded to a discussion of the Propositions on Seminary Training for Priests. Cardinal Meyer and another bishop were the only speakers. Last evening at dinner the Cardinal told us that the matter of seminary training was going to come up and that he was anxious to present his views. Later that evening, His Eminence climbed the three floors of stairs to our rooms and shared with Bishop O'Donnell and myself the intervention he had prepared.

The Cardinal, a former seminary professor in Milwaukee where a good number of our Chicago priests were trained, felt that, "the priest is first of all a man, and to become a good priest he must first be a good man and a good Christian. There is no good priest where there are lacking good human qualities." In other words, the Cardinal would like to see coupled with the Spiritual formation of the seminarian, more emphasis on the human formation of future priests.

And he went on to explain to us that although what he was proposing could apply to most any vocation in life, the sanctity and spirituality that is expected of the priest does not make up for the human deficiencies that may be part of a person's character.

On the floor of St. Peter's the next day, Cardinal Meyer not only brought out the thoughts he had shared with us at home, but added that the Propositions, although generally good, ought to say something about adapting seminary training to local circumstances and needs. I recall, as a seminarian, how isolated we were from what was going on in the great city of Chicago in which I would someday serve as a priest. I feel, and I think this is what the Cardinal may have had in mind, that at some time during the seminarians study years, there ought to be a period of apprenticeship in a parish setting.

November 17, 1964

We've moved into the final week of this session of Vatican II. Yesterday morning there were groans in St. Peter's when the Secretary announced that we may have to go into double sessions, mornings and afternoons if we are to finish the work ahead of us. Many of us have gotten used to those afternoon siestas, what with the ever present local wine accompanying our meals. But then, we Americans have been griping about the short work days of the Council. So you see, that "do as the Romans do" has its limitations as also its advantages!

This morning there was applause when Archbishop Felici, the Council's Secretary, announced that after some deliberation, the Moderators of the Council decided that there would be no afternoon sessions but that the morning meetings may have to be extended beyond the lunch hour. We were also asked to be patient during the long series of final votes that would have to be taken on the many texts that we had debated.

Much of the day's discussion centered on two topics, the continuation of debate on seminary training of future priests and the new text on Christian education. Cardinal Spellman of New York was the first to speak on the latter document, Cardinal Ritter of St. Louis followed him, as did Archbishop Cody of New Orleans.

Cardinal Spellman told us bishops in Council that the intent of the Declaration on Christian Education is "to affirm the rights of parents to choose the schools they wish for their children." His Eminence went on to say that since our Catholic schools serve the public purpose of popular education, the fact that they may be religious in their orientation, should not exclude them from some measure of public support. He insisted that as a consequence of that choice parents should not be subjected to unjust economic burdens and he went so far as to suggest that, "since it is the function of the state to facilitate civil freedoms, justice and equity demand that a due measure of public aid be available to parents to support the schools to which they send their children."

The schema on Education which was first presented to us in the beginning of this third session of Vatican II consisted of a set of propositions. Given the fate of earlier documents that were confined to propositions, the Education Commission itself saw to it that a more comprehensive text would be presented to the bishops. Cardinal Ritter made reference to this fact when he rose to say the Council needs to produce a document on education not only "worthy of the Council but of real and genuine values to men of good will everywhere."

The schema itself contains language like: "Parents and the Church have the inalienable right to educate their children and to start schools . . . parents have the right to entrust their children to schools of their own free choice . . . civil society, without prejudice to its own rights, has the responsibility to help parents discharge their duty in this regard." And finally, the schema speaks of the "serious obligation of parents to see to the religious education of all their children who are not getting a formal religious education in a school."

November 20, 1964

The meeting yesterday exploded in controversy and Cardinal Meyer was perturbed. It all came about when Cardinal Tisserant, presiding over yesterday's meeting, announced in the name of the Council Presidency of which Meyer is a member, that the vote on the document on Religious Liberty would be postponed until the next session of the Council.

Not only was that a contradiction of an announcement made by the Secretary General that a vote would be taken, but Cardinal Meyer said "the members of the Council Presidency were not consulted!" Very much agitated, he went into a huddle with Cardinal Ritter of St. Louis, Leger of Montreal, Canada and Alfrink of the Netherlands. They decided that Ritter, and Leger, would seek an audience with the Holy Father in an effort to forestall delay on a vote for the Religious Liberty document.

At the same time that the Cardinals were mapping out their strategy, pandemonium reigned throughout the Council Hall. Bishops were milling about trying to assess the situation. A paper began to circulate among them that turned out to be a petition to the Holy Father seeking his assurance of a vote on the Liberty schema. The Pope, however, had refused to intervene.

After all, religious freedom was being denied in certain countries and we in America have had long and hard debates about the relations between Church and State. Cardinal Meyer, speaking for the majority of the American bishops, insisted that the text was acceptable to them for three reasons: first, because "the world expected the church to make a statement on religious freedom;" second, the text did make it clear that "the act of faith must be freely made;" and third, such a statement would "make clear the Church's mission." It would prove that the faith was not to be spread by violence.

In the Council itself there were ultra-conservative bishops, blind to what was happening in many parts of the world who would opt for a "simple declaration on religious liberty" that would state the reasons for religious freedom without striving to justify the need of it. Only those bishops insisted that governments had a right to intervene in religious matters. Apparently they were blind to what was happening in the Communist-dominated countries where governments were actively engaged in suppressing religion and religious beliefs.

The following morning, the last working day of this session, a kind of calm and spirit of resignation prevailed. After the usual round of reports on the status of other documents, Cardinal Tisserant rose to tell us that on orders from the Pope, the Religious Liberty schema would be the first document to be considered in the next session of Vatican II. He explained that the newness of the re-drafted text required study and that we ought not rush into a vote.

Please note that I have not reported on the many speeches that were made on the contents of the Religious Liberty document. Not much was said that was different from the reports I made to you in previous letters on the subject. What the bishops wanted was a final vote on a completed schema which was denied them. A vote on a document that would probably be called "the American schema."

But I should tell you that, despite the confusion of the last days of our session, we bishops managed to have obtained the overwhelmingly positive vote on what will be considered the document of Vatican II, that on the Nature of the Church. We also accepted the declaration on Catholic schools for voting and listened to the last document that was placed on the floor for discussion, that on the sacrament of Matrimony.

We also approved the declaration on the Church's relations with non-Christians which includes a strong statement on the Jews. Tomorrow there will be the solemn closing of this third session of Vatican II and I'll probably report on that after I get back home next week. Monsignor Marcinkus, an American priest attached to the Vatican and who lives with us at the "Chicago House" here in Rome, has arranged for a TWA charter flight for fifty or more of us bishops.

Between Third Session and Fourth Session

November 27, 1964 - September 7, 1965

November 27, 1964

Again, may I say, it's good to be back home. We had a nice flight directly to O'Hare Airport. Most of the bishops on our charted flight were from the middle-west and so they lost little time in making connection flights to their dioceses.

November 21st, the closing day of the Third Session of Vatican II, what a day that was! We witnessed, after three years of debate and vote, the official acceptance and proclamation by Pope Paul VI of the schema on the Nature of the Church, officially now, the Dogmatic Constitution on the Church. Probably the most important of the documents of Vatican II, that Constitution will effect the government and mission of the Church for a long time into the future.

Also approved and promulgated was the Decree on Ecumenism as well as the Decree on the Catholic Eastern Churches. Come next January we'll celebrate the traditional Week of Prayer for Christian Unity. Without doubt, the new Decree which gives us further guidelines on Catholic participation in the ecumenical movement will, we hope, encourage Catholics to greater effort for Christian Unity and especially pray for it.

On a personal level, I'll be very much involved in that quest for Christian Unity. I've already been asked to serve with a group of theologians in the dialogue with the Episcopal Church as well as the dialogue with the Disciples of Christ. The request comes because of my past experience in working with various church groups in New York.

I should tell you that the solemnity of the closing of the third session of Vatican II also included two announcements by the Pope. In the course of the ceremony, Paul VI proclaimed Mary as the "Mother of the Church." The Pope also emphasized that the Council would come to a definitive conclusion in the fourth session next year. There was some speculation that a fourth session could start as early as next March. We'll see . . .

And, in a surprise move the Holy Father changed the Eucharistic fast regulations, reducing the time of fasting from solid foods before Communion from three hours to one hour.

As we move now toward the Christmas holidays just a month away and into the beginning of a New Year, diocesan and parish duties may not give me much opportunity to write these letters. Many of you tell me you have been looking forward to reading. There will be brief Sunday reports on our progress in bringing about the liturgical changes initiated by Vatican II, and again, my more personal involvement in the administration of our parish. However, as we move more deeply into winter and a bit of slack in the activities of an auxiliary bishop, I'll be back with more letters. The homework and preparation for the fourth and last session of the Second Vatican Council have already begun. I'll try to keep you abreast.

For now, just this brief report of an interview I witnessed with Bishop Fulton Sheen just before we left for home. Asked about his impressions of the Council, he said in his own inimitable way: "Pope John did what the Risen Lord did. The Church has been behind closed doors for centuries. He said, 'Open the doors! There is a world waiting for salvation. Go into it!'" And the bishop went on to quote a verse from the Apocalypse, "I have set before you an open door, and let no man close it."

With that quotation, Bishop Sheen must have in mind the ideological divisions that surfaced on the floor of St. Peter's when certain prelates pressed for their narrow and sometimes ultra-conservative views on texts we were debating. In contrasting the minority and majority views, the good bishop gave this interesting response, "The Council needs both tendencies, and so does the whole Church. The minority group softened the ideas of the majority and this will give the latter balance, make their definitions more precise and prevent them from throwing out the baby with the bath."

On the other hand, the majority group gave a breath of fresh air to the stuffy atmosphere of the past centuries, enlarged the vision of those who live close to the Mediterranean and made them conscious that the men and women outside the Church are not enemies but friends."

Oh yes, and another thing I liked was the bishop's capsule description of the document on the Church. He said with those piercing eyes and arms gesturing into the distance, "Priests, and this includes bishops, will no longer be like gasoline station attendants caring only for the regular clients who come in weekly for refueling. They will, together with their faithful, need to be explorers digging for the Holy Spirit in the souls of their fellowmen. The doors have been opened wide, much too wide to be closed again."

December 10, 1964

There's a bit of a lull in diocesan and parish activity so I'm back at the desk again with a letter that you might describe as a kind of quick review of that document on the Church which many of us feel will be the most memorable achievement of the Second Vatican Council and which will launch a totally new approach to the way we will think of Church. The faith will not change but the practical conception of what the Church is and does and of how to be a

Christian in today's world will grow on new horizons that could at long last make real our Lord's words, "go forth therefore and make all nations my disciples, baptize everywhere and teach all men to observe what I have commanded you" (Mt. 28/19).

That Constitution which provides solid ground for that kind of growth and the enrichment of our own faith can be summed up this way:

It brings us Catholics to a more biblical understanding of the Church as a community of love in which God communicates the great love He has for us and for our salvation.

It restores the concept of the Church as a People of God in which all of us together share responsibility, by virtue of our baptism, for the work and mission of the Church on earth.

Bishops are no longer presented in that Constitution as mere administrators, but as pastors and leaders more respectful of the role of the clergy and laity in the Church.

And there's that chapter that calls all of us to a holiness of life. What better way to witness the presence of Jesus in our lives, what better familiarity with Him who is our Light, as the first words of the Constitution say, "the Christ who is the Light of the World."

January 6, 1965

As I indicated in one of my mid-November letters to you last year, the final weeks of the third session of Vatican II were full of anxieties. To put it in the colloquial, the bishops got a bit "fidgety" not only with the pace of Council work but probably more so because of frustration over the way their interventions were sometimes ignored at the higher levels. At least, there was not always clear reason given for one-sided changes in some re-drafted texts returned to us for vote. The atmosphere was especially strained as we moved into areas of shared responsibility for the work and mission of the Church.

Some of us, familiar with "the Roman way of doing things" shrugged off apprehensiveness or even disappointment. Others of us brought up in a democracy wondered what was happening to Pope John's Council of Openness and Freedom of Expression. At the Vatican, it's hard to pin things down because one is never sure whether the decisions made somewhere, by someone, have been made responsibly. That sounds harsh, I know, but since public opinion cannot act as a corrective how one can bring judgment into balance.

I've a reason for writing in this vein. Most often in my letters to you I was up front, on stage, and rarely hinted at the back of the scenes drama that is, I suppose, part of any human activity. But there it was, at the highest levels of your Church, bishops mistrusting other bishops. And there it will be when a wholly new concept of Church administration labeled "collegiality" or shared responsibility comes center stage in a future Church.

In Rome, for instance, where the Pope as head of the Church will be expected to consult with delegations of bishops from all parts of the world, in the diocese, where the bishop will need to respond in a new way in his role to teach, sanctify and govern, and at the parish level, where your priest will ask you to share with him concern for the spiritual and temporal welfare of the souls under his care.

Really that term "shared responsibility" is not new. A venerable and ancient writer of Church history, St. Cyprian, said this, "When God permits me to be in your midst, we will treat in common of the things that have been done, or are to be done, with the respect that we owe one another."

Let's start at the top. Last November 12th, a Thursday morning, we bishops in the Council were uptight about what would happen with chapter three of the Constitution on the Church wherein we considered, as a college of bishops (a theological phrase), our relations with the Pope as head of the Church. Vatican II coined that new word as far as that relationship was concerned – collegiality.

Do you know, that ever since the twelve apostles gathered around Jesus, they became conscious that they were members of a closely knit community in common possession of special powers given them by Jesus Christ. They formed the first college of bishops.

One evening at dinner, Father Barnabas Mary Ahearn, who was one of the advisors to Cardinal Meyer on scriptural matters, explained that word collegiality from Scripture. It was an interesting insight into a complicated matter that, as I hinted earlier, caused much discussion and even hard feelings at the Council.

Father Ahearn's explanation indicated that the words "college" and "collegiality" are not found in the Bible but that their meaning can be implied from the way our Lord related to His apostles and they toward each other. " It can be clearly shown", said Father Ahearn "that our Lord founded the Church on the Twelve Apostles and intended this collegiality to perdure." He gave these examples:

Jesus chose the "Twelve" whom we refer to as "apostles." In the early Church the term "apostle" was widely used to designate preachers endowed with special powers. As you know, Jesus grouped these men intimately around him to be the foundation of the Church. Twelve men singled out from all others that would represent that Church in its reality and serve as its bond of unity. And you do remember that Jesus put Peter at the head of this apostolic group.

Father Ahearn went on to demonstrate that, "it was an incontestable fact that the Twelve functioned as a group in the early history of the Church. Their first act after the Ascension of Christ was to fill the place left vacant by the infidelity of Judas. They chose Matthias to complete their number and share their office.

When the first conflict arose in the early Church about imposing Jewish law (circumcision) on gentile Christians coming from paganism, the apostles met in the first Council of the Church, in Jerusalem, to find a peaceful solution to the problem. This practice of facing crisis, or responding to the needs of the Church world-wide, has persisted throughout the centuries up to our day in what is Vatican II, the 21st Council in the long history of the Church."

Our concern last November 12th, therefore, was that there are so many theological subtleties in this area of collegiality or shared responsibilities that we wondered how the new consultation process with the Pope, the Pope with bishops, and bishops among themselves, would turn out.

But this was made clear: first, that the Pope has full, supreme and universal power over the Church; second, the Episcopal college, which is the successor of the college of apostles, in both teaching and pastoral government is to be understood with its head the Pope and never without the head. It also has supreme and full power over the universal Church but this power cannot be used without the consent of the Pope. Note how our documents of Vatican II had to be approved and promulgated by the Pope.

My next letter will deal with that concept of collegiality or shared responsibility at the diocesan and parish levels.

January 12, 1965

One of the documents I did not report to you about was our discussion of the role of bishops – The Pastoral Office of Bishops in the Church – with the feeling that you might not be interested in the technicalities that spell out the bishop's role as head of the diocese. That document, as well as the Dogmatic Constitution on the Church, spells out the bishop's obligation to share responsibility in his teaching, governing and sanctifying role as bishop.

In 1906, the saintly Pope Pius X stated what had been Church policy for centuries going back to the Council of Trent in 1545 when that Council officially "clericalized" the Church. He said "the Church is by its very nature an unequal society; it comprises two categories of persons, the pastors and the flocks. The hierarchy alone moves and controls, the duty of the multitude is to suffer itself to be governed and to carry out in a submissive spirit the orders of those in control."

It was, as my friend and classmate, Bishop Primeau, factually put it one day in St. Peter's when we were talking about the role of the laity in the Church, that it is their sole role was "to pray, pay and obey!"

I remember that kind of authoritarian clericalism that guarantees uniformity, power and privilege. I lived through that in the early years of my priesthood at both the diocesan and parish levels. Clericalism created a chain of command that was rigid, that demanded something close to blind obedience. Once upon a time it worked.

With Vatican II a new and exciting dimension was introduced that would change the long tradition of clerical dominance.

Our first positive step in that direction came when the majority of bishops at the Council defied certain entrenched and conservative bishops who would delineate the structure of the Church in pyramidal form with the Pope at the top, followed by his bishops and priests and the laity at the base of that pyramid. Instead we defined the Church in the Old Testament and early Christian concept as a People of God in which shared responsibility became a theological principle which says that every member of the Church has the right and duty to assist the Church, offering time and talent, so that its mission will become more effective.

That document on the Office of Bishops in the Church speaks not only of the diocesan curia, the Chancery Office, or those closest to the bishop in his daily work, but of those who will be expected to consult and collaborate with him. For instance, episcopal vicars who are assigned to specific areas of the diocese, a board of consultors that will help make decisions on temporal matters like the acquisition of property, the building of churches and the like; and priests' councils or senates that will deliberate in areas of specific concern to priests and even on diocesan matters that may or may not be in the purview of the diocesan pastoral council which would be made up of priests, religious and laity. The latter consultative body was strongly recommended by the Pastoral Constitution on the Church.

On the surface you will recognize a whole new bureaucracy that may challenge the genius of the bishop who will need to see to the coordination of all those consultative and collaborative bodies.

The same holds true for the pastor at the parish level. The documents of Vatican II strongly recommend the establishment of the Parish Council made up of people who are members and serve the parish at various levels: A Board of Education, a Finance Council, a Building and Grounds Committee, etc.

January 22, 1965

If you're a weekly subscriber to our archdiocesan paper, then you may be ahead of me. Last Friday, His Eminence, Cardinal Meyer, addressed a group of Protestant ministers and gave them a splendid expose of the Council's document on Ecumenism, as well as a bit of insight on the "Nature of Church."

The talk to the ministers at the Theological Seminary on the campus of the University of Chicago was preparation of a pastoral letter the Cardinal will be sending to all of us priests regarding the implementation throughout the Archdiocese of the Second Vatican Council document on

Ecumenism. At the heart of the Cardinal's talk was the approach to dialogue with our Christian brethren based on the theological virtues of faith, hope and charity, a capsulization of the many interventions that accompanied our debates in the Council. In that spirit His Eminence defined ecumenism this way:

"The word 'ecumenical' should describe an attitude of mind attuned in faith to a visible unity, not only of love and hope, but also of faith among all people who confess Christ as Lord."

The Cardinal reminded his listeners that Christ himself desired this unity when at the Last Supper he prayed that, "Father, it is not for these alone (those closest to me) that I pray, but for those also who through their words put their faith in me; may they all be one, as we are one." (Jn. 17-20, 21)

"Ecumenism," the Cardinal urged, "consists in our really listening to Christ's prayer for unity, and to His promise that this unity is really possible. We must believe that Christ desires this unity with all His heart, and that we have the obligation to work for it."

Then in a more technical manner, the Cardinal described unity as something more than just brotherhood or friendliness, something even more than a genuine Christian love and hope for mutual salvation. What we must seek is a genuine unity in faith, something like what Pope Paul VI said to us at the opening of the second session of the Council:

"This mysterious and visible unity can be realized only in one faith, in partaking in the same sacraments, and by a suitable link with a single supreme leadership of the Church."

Now those are difficult words and I remember how some of the Protestant observers at the Council were disappointed in hearing them. But the truth must come out. We need to be honest. We cannot build up any false hopes with empty words. Again, Pope Paul said it better:

"The time has come when the truth regarding the Church of Christ should be examined, coordinated and expressed."

The Cardinal pursued that direction for honesty by quoting the Dean of the Theological Seminary in New York who said, "This new community, this body, the Church, is given so high a place in the New Testament that biblical studies themselves have demolished the religious individualism of much of modern Protestantism."

You do know that I have personally been involved for some time in dialogue with certain of the Protestant churches. That is why I hope you will forgive me if I pursue this subject of ecumenism further in future letters to you. You, too, will better understand my closeness to the ministers of the other churches in our area and the reason for their participation in some of our church functions.

By the way, news has reached me that Father John Courtney Murray, the American Jesuit theologian who was of such great assistance to our Cardinal in the debate on Religious Freedom in the Council, became ill while visiting his gravely ill sister. He died two days after he entered a hospital in Jamaica, New York having suffered a heart attack in a taxi.

January 27, 1965

This whole matter of Ecumenism is even more breathtaking, it seems to me, if we think about the very words of Jesus Himself, when He compares the unity of the Church to the unity between the persons of the Blessed Trinity, and the absolute unity of God Himself. Those words I quoted in my last letter to you from St. John's gospel (Jn. 17/21) bring that out beautifully.

Cardinal Meyer in his talk at the Chicago Theological Seminary just about a week ago emphasized that truth when he said: "Obviously this marvelous union can only be the work of the Holy Spirit since the Church is made up of weak, sinful human beings filled with contradictory tendencies, with selfishness and blindness. In its human side, the Church is indeed liable to disruptive tendencies. It has had terrible periods of decline and suffering."

How often we talked about that human side of the Church. The Cardinal, I recall, as you may remember from some of my past letters, spoke publicly of that weak side of the Church and its members when he intervened in the Council discussion of the Nature of the Church and again, when we were discussing the role of the priesthood in today's world.

More recently, while sitting next to the Cardinal at a dinner for one of our priest jubilarians, His Eminence, probably looking into the groups of priests and laity that evening mused: "I wonder about the future of the Church and how all of our work at the Council, the implementation of those documents, will affect the spirit of these people."

Fresh from the accolades he received after his speech on ecumenism, he went on to say, "many of those people out there, clergy and laity, will feel that we've watered down doctrine and belief with our new attitude toward the Protestant churches. I've already had letters complaining that the new liturgy, the Mass, is cold, like Protestant services, that we're aping them too much."

At our Board meeting of the Bishops' conference I attended last week in Washington, one of the bishops asked if I had received any reaction from clergy or laity about sitting down with Protestants and discussing theology, dialoguing with them. I had not, but the good bishop said he was the recipient of some nasty letters from people in his diocese. It could be that our Cardinal's concerns may be prophetic of the future.

But to get back to his talk at the University, and this is a point I wish our Catholic clergy and laity will understand.

It hinges on what I said earlier, "One of the solid signs," said the Cardinal, "among the leaders in dialogue is that unity cannot be achieved by any compromise in matters of faith and doctrine." I know that for sure from the many hours I sat at the dialogue table. There can be no compromise of the truth. "Truth is an absolute," said the Cardinal, "which cannot be diminished, as witnessed by so many martyrs."

One of the characteristics of dialogue, as I see it, and as we're practicing it at our meetings, is in trying to understand the position of the other side and to have our doctrine understood by them. We do have much to learn from each other. Pope Pius XII once said that we need to get to the sources, to return to the Bible. By the way, you will notice as you read the Council documents that they are replete with quotations from the Scriptures. And you know, our Protestant friends are pretty familiar with the Scriptures, something we have neglected in our Church.

February 3, 1965

As I move about the archdiocese these days especially when I am with my fellow priests at confirmation, interest centers on certain events of the Council of Vatican II in Rome. Frequently Cardinal Meyer is the focus of those conversations, especially the impact he has had on the work of the Council, but here at home, what for many is a surprise, is his zeal in interpreting and implementing the documents and decrees of Vatican II.

Rumor has it that the Cardinal is not well. Matter of fact, that is true and we are worried about him. While we were in Rome last fall His Eminence complained of persistent headaches. One evening he asked me for the name of the American doctor who was trained in the United States but was practicing medicine not far from where we lived. I had just been over a cold and mentioned at dinner one evening that the doctor had helped me. Apparently those head-aches are recurring.

As is normal, I suppose, the media's concentration on the sensational often sets the theme for those conversations I was encountering at confirmations. I was asked several times "Did the Cardinal blow his top over that Religious Liberty thing?" *"Time* magazine," said one priest, "de-scribed His Eminence as being 'livid' with anger." Another said, "The *Trib* reported that he was furious and that he was delegated to see the Pope about something having to do with voting.

I found myself coupling those uncharacteristic descrip-tions of the Cardinal's personality with the surprise my brother priests expressed in the way he was moving on the Council documents in the archdiocese. What really was at the center of all those conversations was the observation of the noticeable change of temperament many saw in His Eminence.

If I may put it succinctly, with Vatican II Cardinal Meyer came unto his own. He took on a new image for the priests and laity of Chicago. Prior to the Council the Cardinal's ret-icence and reserve were considered by many as a throw-back to his German ancestry. One priest asked me: "Did His Eminence ever tell a joke?" Once, at a public function, the Cardinal arranged for me to sit next to him with the pretext that we had business to discuss. As we moved into the first courses of the dinner, he confided that he was uncomfortable with sitting next to someone who had too many cocktails. He was not one for idle conversation.

With his emerging leadership in the Council proceedings and the reports on the nature and frequency of his inter-ventions especially as they related to priests and the priest-hood, many observed that indeed, Chicago was blessed with a good shepherd and a highly intellectual leader.

A week ago the Cardinal invited me to his home and asked that I arrange a meeting for all the clergy of the archdiocese. He was anxious to give a report of our last session in Rome and to officially support the work my commission on the liturgy was doing. I was a bit shocked at his appearance. His face was drawn and his eyes gave one the impression that he was suffering. He admitted that his headaches were back and getting worse. However, he told me to go ahead with plans for the meeting with his priests.

I shall never forget that meeting in the auditorium of Resurrection Parish on the near west side. I met His Eminence at his car and as I was leading him through the rear door to the stage he turned to me and said: "Bishop, I'm not at all up to giving the kind of talk I was hoping for to our priests. Will you please take over after I give an opening prayer?"

Believe me, I was not prepared for what followed. As soon as the Cardinal approached center stage toward the microphone, applause broke out and the priests gave His Eminence a standing ovation that must have lasted at least ten minutes. The Cardinal was obviously so moved that he asked me to say the prayer he had prepared for the meeting. I suspected that he was reluctant to display the emotion that came upon him so suddenly.

After the prayer, and with a bit of hesitation, the Cardinal rose from the chair behind a desk we had arranged for him on the stage and approached the microphone. Again, but this time applause moved our sometimes stoic and reticent Cardinal to tears. In a few brief but moving words the Cardinal asked forgiveness of the priest and begged to be excused, but not after he told us how much he admired our work and our zeal. His parting words, again interrupted by applause, were: "Please make the Council come alive."

I must confess that there was a lump in my throat and prayerful concern as I led His Eminence back to his car.

March 8, 1965

You will recall that in one of my letters to you last January on the subject of Ecumenism, I promised further reflection on Cardinal Meyer's scholarly talk to a group of Protestant ministers at the Chicago Theological Seminary of the campus of the University of Chicago. Understandably, the subject matter of the last few letters impeded that promise. I would like to think that, given our Cardinal's present state of health, he would encourage me to share his thoughts with you.

Prior to giving reasons for a "well-founded hope" that there is much that we can do to improve our relationships with the other Christian churches, Cardinal Meyer made clear, "that the future of the ecumenical movement in America will depend on how we harmonize a repentant acknowledgement of our divisions with a realistic recognition of our pluralism."

His Eminence then went on to place within the context of our religious-socio-political tensions in America the much needed theological clarification of the concept to religious liberty.

In the theological arena he mentioned such of our own doctrines as the Mass and the Real Presence of Christ in the Eucharist, our veneration of the Blessed Virgin Mary and our teaching on Purgatory.

In the field of morals, His Eminence emphasized our differences on birth control and the various forms of gambling that are in the limelight today, things like bingo and other games of chance that are so much a part of our parish fund-raising efforts.

In our social relationships, he mentioned the question of the place of religion in education and the related problem of state-aid for our parochial schools.

In that whole area of our differences, as I mentioned earlier, that concept of religious liberty needs to be clarified.

After quoting the encyclical of Pope John XXIII, "Peace on Earth," which states that, "Every human being has the right to honor God according to the dictates of an upright conscience and the right to profess his religion privately and publicly," the Cardinal recalled the struggle he went through with the Religious Liberty document at our last session the Council. He acknowledged that "It was just as well that the document did not get through the last session since there was lack of time to do it justice. I am looking forward to its discussion the next session and I know that the text can be perfected."

May I at this point tell you that there is much more to this religious liberty thing than appears on the surface. At the Council, if you remember some of the contents of my letters to you, there was a great deal of controversy over how that idea of freedom in religious matters can be abused. If you don't mind, I'll get into that another time. At the moment I'd like to conclude my report on Cardinal Meyer's talk on Ecumenism.

After developing the reasons for the "well-founded" hope we have a dialogue with our Protestant brethren, His Eminence provided direction by stating "that there is no better beginning than the exercise of charity. Whatever truly unites us to Christ must unite us also to those who are in Christ. Such charity must remove from us and our hearts those enemies of the true ecumenical spirit which are complacency, and resentment and fear – the complacency of the Pharisee, the resentment of the laborers in the vineyard, the fear of the one-talent servant."

March 18, 1965

If I were to give a title to this letter it could be along these lines: What happens to the documents the bishops worked on in Rome during the Council and what happens when they get back home? There is, therefore, a two-pronged theme to this letter. One, a report on the special commissions that were authorized to provide directives for the implementations of those documents which the Council has already approved, and two, something of what your bishops are doing here at home to follow through on those directives from Rome.

One of the very first documents the bishops completed in Rome and which the Holy Father officially promulgated in December 1963, was that on the liturgy. Another was on the Means of Social Communication. It is about the former document that I write today.

We've had two important "follow-through" communications from Rome on that matter of the liturgy: one, a special letter from Pope Paul VI called "Motu Proprio," a kind of administrative directive, in which he urged that "all Christians, especially priests, study the Constitution on the Liturgy and be prepared to wholeheartedly and loyally put it into effect." And further, the Holy Father urged that, "bishops set about at once to teach their people the power and interior worth of the liturgy." For the past year we've done just that with the help of our Archdiocesan Commission on the Liturgy which I head.

The other communication from Rome on the liturgy that came to us last September was, An Instruction on the Proper Implementation of the Constitution on the Sacred Liturgy. You'll find the chapter headings in that Instruction, taken for the most part out of specific articles in the Constitution, informative enough:

Liturgical Formation of the Clergy (Art. 15, 16, 18), for Religious and the Laity (Art. 19). The Competent Authority in Liturgical Matters, (Art. 22); Bible Services; the Use of the Vernacular etc.

As for our part, Bishop O'Donnell and myself? Well, we've been moving around the diocese to special meetings, and what with confirmations, many opportunities to speak on a one-to-one basis with our fellow priests about the

Council in general and the Implementation of the Liturgy document in particular. But it is especially about our Cardinal's role that I would like to tell you about.

After we returned from Rome in 1962 and through 1963, His Eminence gave reports on the Council not only to our priests at several meetings with them, but also gave a series of lectures to our seminarians at Mundelein.

You, of course, realize that we bishops face a period of anxiety and even tension in implementing the reforms that have come out of the Second Vatican Council. As shepherds and teachers we have the duty to inform and to guide in this new era of freedom. We've had the personal experience, that special kind of glow as participants in the Council and we need now to share that experience and grow with you.

I did report to you on that moving meeting the Cardinal had with his priests at Resurrection Parish some time ago. Here is a short excerpt from a lecture His Eminence gave to our seminarians; it might serve you as a good review of the many things I reported on from Rome.

The Cardinal, in explaining the reasons why he was so anxious to speak to the seminarians said, "I want very badly to bring the Council to life back home." And he went on to say that there were three ways in which he could do this: By recounting the day to day life in Rome, "regaling you with the human incidents, the joys and sorrows of our deliberations; by giving breath and depth to the documents, summarizing them briefly for you, giving heart and sinew to our work, or sharing with you the many ideas and questions you have about Vatican II."

And so the Cardinal went on, choosing to give a very brief history of the three sessions this way.

The first session he called "a search for renewal." This he emphasized, "is what Pope John had in mind. He wanted change in the Church's structure, allowing for more freedom, personal initiative." And, "that new freedom," he explained "has a new dimension as it relates to priest and bishop, bishop to the Pope, and Pope, bishops and priests to the laity." As for "personal initiative," he quoted Pope John who said that, "I must get this soul of mine out of the mud and on the road to heaven."

Since this article is getting a bit long, I'll go into the rest of the Cardinal's talk next week.

March 25, 1965

The second session of Vatican II, Cardinal Meyer described as one that began to discuss "the tools for renewal." Those tools, he described as the documents that had been voted on by the bishops, approved and promulgated by the Pope, and those documents that would be acted upon.

Regarding the Liturgy document, His Eminence not only gave an excellent summary of its chapters and sections, but described it "as the summit of the Church's efforts to proclaim the God in Whom we believe." How the liturgy, with "its emphasis of adaptation to different cultures, its emphasis on the Bible, on the role of the laity in prayer and worship, the simplification of ceremonies, all of these and more, enhanced our prayer life and encourages you, my dear seminarians, to deeper study of that which will be the center of your priestly lives."

The Cardinal went on to describe the document on Social Communications, which like Liturgy, was also approved and promulgated by the Holy Father at the end of our 1963 session. Of that text he said that we "live in a great technological society in which man's right to true and complete information within the limits of justice and charity must be adhered to. An objective moral order . . . itself surpasses and fittingly coordinates all other spheres of human affairs."

As for the third session of the Council, the Cardinal described it as the "search for the Church's identity." "He had in mind the document on the Church that spoke of the 'People of God as a Messianic people who have Christ as their leader.'" He spoke of the new concept of "collegiality in which the Pope with his bishops make up the college to govern the Church . . . of the laity who share in the priestly, prophetical and kingly functions of Christ – how they share in the mission and work of the Church and seek the kingdom of God by engaging in temporal affairs and ordering them according to the plan of God."

His Eminence further described the third session as one full of triumphs and failures. In picturing a "kind of letdown feeling," he referred to our discussions of the Religious Liberty document in which he played such a prominent part and which I described to you in an earlier letter. He told the seminarians that the liberty "text could be considered to be a supreme contribution of the Vatican II Council. The other documents may have less of an immediate impact upon the thinking and believing world – after all, internal as they are, they may assume less importance in the perspective of history."

As for his personal feelings about the transfer of the document to the last and fourth session of the Council, he said "that may be just as well. There was too little time for a full discussion and I look forward to its revival next fall."

His Eminence, in separate talks to his seminarians also touched upon the Council texts on Christian Education, on Religious Life, on Priestly Training and the Life and Ministry of Priests; on the Relationships of the Church to non-Christians, the Role of the Laity in a Renewing Church and other texts that he hoped to take part in during the next and last session of the Council.

The seminarians knew from media reports of the Cardinal's personal and strong feelings about training for the priesthood and priestly ministry. The emotional impact he put into explaining those specific documents on priestly training and ministry evidenced his deep love for the priesthood.

For instance, this is how he expressed his conviction on the role of the Eucharist in the priest's life. When we were working on the first draft of the document on the Priesthood, the Cardinal brought to our attention one evening at dinner a footnote to the document on the "unity of the priesthood." Almost in a meditative way he observed: "It seems to me that no matter how different may be our tasks and apostolate, all of us who are priests find the unity of our lives in the way our priesthood is centered in the Eucharist." He then went on to say that the priesthood makes us 'keepers of the Eucharist' for the good of the people of God."

April 9, 1965

This morning about 10:30 Cardinal Meyer died at the age of 62. Tomorrow morning archdiocesan officials will be meeting to discuss funeral arrangements and the Board of Consultors will vote on the appointment of a temporary Administrator for the Archdiocese.

A sudden and unexpected death is always difficult to accept but even the expected death of our beloved Cardinal brings deep sorrow to all of our hearts. We were prepared for his passing but are even now more concerned about the impact of his death on the archdiocese and the forthcoming session of the Second Vatican Council. His Eminence truly believed that the Council was the work of God and we here at home had great expectations of his leadership in, as he said, "bringing the Council back home."

I will miss the daily trips with him from our home in Rome to St. Peter's when the bishops of the world will gather for the final session of Vatican II. I will miss the sharing of his great mind, the example of a beautiful priestly life, his deep love for the Church. My friend, Cardinal Cushing of Boston wrote and said: "His death deprives the

Church in America of one who, from many points of view, was the greatest churchman of our times. Priest, scholar, shepherd, he was all of that to many of us."

April 15, 1965

By now you know that I had the privilege of celebrating one of the Masses at the Cathedral for His Eminence, the Mass attended by the school children of our Archdiocese. May I share this excerpt from my homily:

"He was a gentle man, like a child understands gentleness.

He was a kind man, like a child understands kindness.

He was a prayerful man, like a child is prayerful.

No fancy words; he knew how to talk to our Lord.

He loved you, good, bad or hurt, because Jesus told us that unless we become as little children, we will not enter the Kingdom of Heaven."

Archbishop Cousins of Milwaukee, who gave the funeral eulogy on Tuesday morning, spoke for all of us when he said: "Cardinal Meyer was a Churchman in the best and broadest sense of the word. The Church, divinely founded, custodian of Christ's doctrine, the authority to be followed with confidence and conviction, was his first and only love, the priesthood, the means to sharing that love with others.

He was strictly objective, keenly analytical and firmly balanced in all his views. His brother bishops were proud of him and their pride was matched by the high esteem of his confreres from every part of the world."

Yes, he seemed reserved, almost shy. In the judgment of some, he was aloof, impersonal, but this was a false impression and one he never intended to create.

I can attest to that. Our Cardinal loved the Church and the faithful who were his flock in Superior, Wisconsin, in Milwaukee and in Chicago. He applied his great mind to the renewal of the Church which Pope John XXIII had asked for, and on returning home from the first session of the Council said: "We are meeting to confront the Church with the modern world and to confront the modern world with the Church."

I sought out an intervention at the Council which His Eminence had made that provides practical application of that observation on the purpose of Vatican II. In our discussion of the schema on the Church he said:

"The schema explains in different ways why the Christians living in the world ought to work for the advancement of the temporal order . . . we should not forget that God offers the hope of glory not just to man's soul, but to his whole person and to the entire world . . . the whole world is not only the means by which redeemed man perfects himself, but is itself the object of redemption, just as our bodies are."

And then I was thinking about the interest Cardinal Meyer had in the schema on the Church in the Modern World, that says so much about our obligation to convert the world to Christ. I was thinking about how much that intervention he made on the Church document which I just quoted applied to a schema he would never see completed.

April 29, 1965

These are busy days for me. April, May, and June are, as you know, confirmation months and there is hardly an evening that I am at home and at my desk where I like to write these letters to you. And what with the death of our Cardinal, Bishop O'Donnell and I will be picking up many of the dates he had in his schedule. Yes, you're right, this reads like I'm getting ready to make excuses for not writing to you more often. There is, however, a promise to be kept and I'll try to continue to be in touch with you as often as I can.

Cardinal Meyer spoke before the Council of Vatican II

thirty-seven times and submitted an unknown number of written interventions. His name is especially revered in connection with the documents on Revelation, Ecumenism, Liturgy, Priestly Life and Ministry, and Religious Liberty.

His Eminence felt that the Dogmatic Constitution on the Church – Lumen Gentium, as we call it in Latin – "was the most important contribution of Vatican Council II." His oral intervention on October 21, 1963 emphasized this concept of the People of God which was written into the final draft. He said:

"In order that our schema may reach the hearts of men today, men who are burdened both by a sense of sin and of their own weakness, my preference is that before the People of God is described as being without stain or wrinkle, we preface this with words that describe the Church as the household of the Father of mercies in which the failings of its prodigal sons are forgiven, their wounds are bound up, their weaknesses are cured, and their needs are answered."

And then he reminded the bishops in St. Peter's of this sentence from the Bible, "I have not come to summon the just, but sinners" (Mk. 2/17). Then he closed to applause on this note:

"The schema should not speak of the privileges of the People of God, but should emphasize very strongly the difficulties of leading a genuinely Christian life."

Cardinal Meyer's viewpoints on the Constitution on the Liturgy surprised many of us. Only later did I learn, when he asked me to head a liturgical commission for the archdiocese and he gave me access to his library, that he was a devout follower of the Benedictine school of liturgy, a great admirer of Virgil Michael, Martin Helriegel, Godfrey Diekmann and other Benedictine priests who pioneered in the movement for changes in the liturgy. The classic work of Father Joseph Jungmann S. J. on the liturgy was heavily marked with the Cardinal's observations.

I recall this intervention the Cardinal made about the use of other languages than Latin in the Liturgy and other sacraments. On October 24, 1962, he made these two points:

"In the first place, with regard to the liturgical language, the norm laid down in this document seems to me to be very good. It expresses a true middle path between various opposing opinions. As to the use of 'popular languages' I like the idea that this decision be first left to the National Episcopal Conference and then to the Holy See for final approval.

In the second place, the breath of power that seems to be attributed to a national liturgical commission, specifically these words, 'to moderate liturgical pastoral action in the entire nation,' does not please me. Let it always be the bishop in his own diocese who is the moderator of liturgical pastoral action under the rule of the Holy See, and not under the rule of some national commission."

Again on November 9, 1962, in the continuing debate of the document on the liturgy, the Cardinal spoke about the Divine Office, the Breviary, as you know it. He opposed the praying of the Office at fixed hours of the day arguing that, "even though that is the ideal, it can scarcely be attained by priests engaged in the active ministry despite their best intentions."

And he made this appeal: "I strongly wish that the Council Fathers would give consideration to the use of the vernacular in the private recitation of the Breviary."

When we were in the midst of the discussion of the schema on the Nature of the Church, its membership and mission, Cardinal Meyer rose to support the delicate and much debated topic of collegiality or shared responsibility. His observations centered on the scriptural foundations for that concept. He recalled that:

"Our Lord Jesus Christ entrusted his Church to a college of twelve apostles. The New Testament contains sayings and actions of Christ which can be interpreted in favor of collegiality and its transmission to the bishops."

And the Cardinal went to make the point that it is also clear from the New Testament that, "the Lord wished that the body of the Twelve endure in the Church until the end of the world." He cited that phrase from scriptures in which the Lord said: "I am with you all days until the consummation of the world." And later, in that long intervention, His Eminence observed that, "after Christ's ascension was the birth of the Church on Pentecost Sunday. Following on St. Peter's revelation and the collegial experience of that day, the Church was born through the collegial action of the Twelve Apostles."

I suspect that Cardinal Meyer's favorite schema of Vatican II was that on Revelation, perhaps because he was by training, example and teaching a scripture scholar. He made several interventions in writing, and three oral ones. Among the latter were two that supported the dual fonts of revelation, scripture and tradition. Of the latter he said:

"Sacred tradition is something living, dynamic, and all-embracing, that is, that it consists not only in doctrinal propositions, but also in the worship and practice of the entire Church."

I wish there were space to develop the whole of the Cardinal's thoughts on Revelation. Much of what he said was honored by the Writing Commission and I'm sure will be preserved in the history of Vatican II and the final document when it is voted on in the next session.

May 6, 1965

I trust that you agree with my pursuit of eulogizing our departed Cardinal Archbishop in recalling his dedicated work during the three sessions of Vatican II which he attended. In this writing I would like to tell you something about his interest in the document on Ecumenism, this over and beyond what I reported to you of the Cardinal's interest in that area earlier this year, and something about his other interventions.

Overall, the declaration on Ecumenism was acceptable to His Eminence except for the way the schema handled the subject of "social peace and religious liberty." On November 20, 1963 he said, "My objection is that the determination of the fact that the conditions for the limitation of religious liberty have been reached is left to the discretion of civil rulers. It is they who are to determine when religious liberty 'seriously contradicts the end of society' and the 'uses' of religious liberty are 'perverse.' Our experience of the subjective way in which civil rulers can decide such matters should warn us to be more prudent here.

I would suggest that social harmony requires that all individuals living in society exercise their right to religious liberty, with moderation, in the interest of social peace and that all have the obligation to practice prudence in this regard. All should respect the religious sincerity of others and not regard differences of religious belief and practice as excuses for violating the moral obligation to treat all citizens with respect, justice and charity."

And in the light of the political situation in our own country the Cardinal added this note to his unusually long intervention:

"Although it is understandable that, in some countries, adherence to a particular religion, regarded as part of a people's historical culture, be required for eligibility to public office, this requirement runs counter to the principle of religious liberty as a civil right. It also runs counter to the political right of the people to choose whoever they believe will best govern them."

Now I should tell you that Cardinal Meyer gave further insights on other documents that would not be of particular interest to you. For that reason, in the interest of space, I am avoiding reference to them.

The only intervention made on the Decree on Priestly

Formation was made by the Cardinal on November 12, 1964 shortly before we were making plans for our return home. You may recall my writing to you about that intervention last year and telling you how disappointed His Eminence was with the "few propositions that treat of so excellent a theme." This is what he said:

"The importance of this schema is such that it can scarcely be exaggerated. So much of what was so admirably said here on the schema on the 'Priestly Life and Ministry' can also be applied to this schema. For the formation of seminarians tends precisely to be a preparation for the priestly life and ministry. We may, on that account, doubt, just as with the former schema, whether our present schema in these few propositions really treats so excellent a theme sufficiently."

The Cardinal then, as former rector of the seminary in Milwaukee, went on for some time to speak of the particular areas necessary for good seminary training with which he was so familiar. As I listened to him, I could sense the emotion that dictated his thoughts. I felt, at one point, that given the present situation of many priests in our country, their sometime problem of knowing who and what they are and what was expected of them, these words seemed prophetic to me:

"The priesthood, although conferred in a sacrament, is, first of all, a grace given freely to an individual for the good of the Church. Whether one uses this grace worthily or unworthily depends on his human cooperation which, with the help of grace, should stand forth. No one can prudently take upon himself the obligations of a priestly life unless he has previously shown the human capacity to bear these obligations and to persevere in fulfilling them."

Well, this will be the last of the reports I will make to you on Cardinal Meyer's contribution to the work of the Second Vatican Council.

The Council's Declaration on the Relationships of the Church to non-Christian Religions was probably inspired by Pope John XXIII. Many of us bishops recalled the Pope's very warm greeting to a Jewish delegation in 1962 when, with outstretched arms he said to that group representing the American Jewish Committee, "I am Joseph, your brother." Another time when the Pope was talking to some leaders of the B'nai B'rith there was this appeal, "You of the Old Testament and we of the New must come closer and closer, as brothers under God, to work for peace throughout the world."

All during our sessions on Ecumenism the subject of our relationships with non-Christians was brought up and often special reference was made to the Jews. Hints abounded that there ought to come out of the Council some kind of statement on anti-Semitism, something of our special kinship with the Jewish religion because of our Lord. On November 8, 1963, the original text of a proposed Declaration was given us bishops in Council titled: "The Relation of Catholics to non-Christians and especially the Jews." And then another text, "Concerning the Jews and non-Christians" was brought to our attention. But it was a third version, simply called a Declaration on the "Relationship of the Church to non-Christian Religions" that was actually debated on the floor of St. Peter's and to which Cardinal Meyer had addressed himself.

Following on an intervention made by Cardinal Spellman of New York who said that we "should confess humbly before the world that Christians too frequently have not shown themselves as true Christians, as faithful to Christ, in their relations with their Jewish brothers, Cardinal Meyer observed that we now have a schema that deals with that matter and I find it satisfactory." However, our Cardinal went on to say that he felt the "earlier text given to us last year dealt with the question of the Jews in a better and more ecumenical fashion." He explained his position this way:

"It is not sufficient, in my judgment, to say that the Church decries and condemns hatred and persecution of the Jews for the simple reason that 'it severely repudiates wrongs done to man whenever they appear.' Justice demands that we give explicit attention to the enormous impact of the wrongs done through the centuries to the Jews. The particular afflictions which the Jewish people have undergone make it imperative that we add a special condemnation of every form of anti-Semitism, as was done in the earlier text when it stated: 'Thus it all the more decries and condemns with maternal sentiments the hatred and persecutions inflicted on the Jews, whether of old or in our times.'"

The Cardinal then, in another section of his intervention concluded that:

"Those lines in the previous text, as they stand, admonish people never to speak of the Jews as a reprobate race, and 'not to blame the Jews of our day for what happened in the passion of the Christ.'"

Overall, Cardinal Meyer drew on the treasury of his scriptural expertise by insisting that, "it is a fact of history that many Christians have not always properly acknowledged the role of the Jewish people in the economy of salvation – they have, and in fact demeaned it. It is our task to remove the cause of this failing and the remind the faithful of Sacred Scripture's unambiguous teaching about this people . . . that from the Jewish people were born Christ's mother, the Virgin Mary, and the Apostles, the foundation and pillars of the Church, and those many early Christians who first gave the teaching of Christ to the world."

The last intervention Cardinal Meyer made at the Second Vatican Council was perhaps the one that capped his brilliant record at the Council – the one on Religious Freedom which unfairly characterized him as an "explosive person." You are familiar, from earlier letters I wrote to you, about his disappointment that the schema on Religious Freedom was not voted on and approved at the end of the third session of the Council, and that in conformity with the rules of the Council, its further debate and final decision was to be the first topic for discussion in a fourth session in the fall of 1965.

For the record here are excerpts from the Cardinal's presentation on the Religious Liberty schema:

"Men of our day long for the Church to promote rather than to fear religious freedom. This longing rises from a certain common experience by which, on the one hand, they have noted religious persecutions wherever the unlimited power of the State prevailed, and, on the other, they have observed religion flourishing in regions where peaceful coexistence of various religious groups is allowed.

The Church needs to give an example to governments of the world on how to conduct themselves in this delicate area of religious freedom."

True religion consists essentially not so much in the display of external belonging to a religion, but rather to conscious, free and generous submission of a person to the will of the Creator."

And in a final point, Cardinal Meyer said, "this affirmation of religious freedom is essential for the fruitful dialogue with non-Catholics."

September 7, 1965

In a few days, Bishop O'Donnell and I will be accompanying our new Archbishop to Rome for the fourth and final session of Vatican II. We, of course, are wondering how it will be with our new "boss" at our Chicago House of Studies. There have been changes. And judging from the amount of work material I have received, we are going to be very busy from now until the Council ends on December 8th.

And speaking about this fourth session, I should interject that Cardinal Meyer had a great deal to do with bringing about that session, which, unfortunately he would never attend. About midway through the third session the question arose whether it would be possible to bring the Council to a close at the end of that session. The American bishops were divided. Archbishop Krol, serving the Secretariat for the Council, argued in favor of seeking an end to Vatican II, but the majority, under the leadership of Cardinal Meyer, moved in favor of our returning to Rome for a fourth and possible final session of the Council in 1965.

I had a letter from Monsignor Howard, Rector of our House on via Sardegna, advising me that my old room was waiting my arrival at the Collegio Santa Maria del Lago, that's the formal name of our residence in Rome. He also reminded me that the three students who had been with us in the past had completed their studies had returned to the archdiocese for assignments, that since we buried Verna, the former housekeeper who mothered us to no end in the past, we would be having a new "lady of the House" to supervise our needs.

Monsignor Howard also assured me that he would have all my personal things that had been stored away since the last session ready for me in my room. He chided me about "those antiquated golf clubs" I left behind and suggested that I bring over a new pair of golf shoes.

So it will be like coming back home to Rome and the excitement of new adventure. As I said earlier, there will be a lot of hard work ahead. After all, in the past three years the Council had given the universal Church just five of the sixteen documents that will apparently become a part of the history of Vatican II.

Would we ever catch up was in the temper of our minds. We realized that the Church and the world waiting for our decision on documents like, Religious Liberty, the Training of Priests, the Renewal of Religious Life, the Decree on the Pastoral Office of Bishops, Christian Education, the unfinished document of Revelation, the Pastoral Constitution on the Church in the Modern World and four other decrees.

The moment I get unpacked and settled in Rome, I'll be in touch with you about what I suspect will be a new atmosphere in our Chicago House and the heightened anticipation that will be expected because this will be our last meeting on the Council.

The Fourth Session
of Vatican Council II

September 14, 1965 - December 8, 1965

September 16, 1965

The opening of the fourth and last session of Vatican II on Tuesday was, as I expected, a majestic display of ritual and color. The Council itself is now a testing ground for the changes it asked for when it enacted in 1963 the Constitution on the Liturgy. The Mass was concelebrated by twenty-six bishops and the Pope.

As was the practice here with every opening of our meetings we began with Mass which was followed by the procession and the solemn enthronement of the Gospel. Tuesday's official opening was a bit different.

The enthronement ceremony, instead of being a separate procession, was incorporated into the first part of Mass with what is called the Introit Antiphon and its Psalm verses which we sang. The concelebrants, instead of standing behind the Pope or below the altar, and contrary to the regulations issued earlier this year, stood at all four sides of the altar, thus obscuring the Pope who was the main celebrant.

Another variation I noticed was that instead of the deacon, one of the concelebrants read the gospel. There was no homily. The Pope read his speech at the end of Mass.

What excited us about the Holy Father's speech was not so much the surprise announcement of his intention to create an Episcopal synod, but clarification of his position regarding that concept of collegiality which troubled us in the last session and caused the delay in the publication of the amended document on the Church.

I remember Cardinal Meyer telling us at table one evening that despite the fact that the theological commission had finished its work on the document, a small, but powerful minority group was finding it hard to make up his mind about how much authority he was willing to share with his bishops.

So it was that Pope Paul VI not only acceded to the wishes of his bishops assembled in Council in the matter of shared responsibility but the very next day issued a formal decree or "Motu Proprio," spelling out details of such an Episcopal synod through which bishops, by virtue of their consecration, are co-responsible for the teaching and ruling of the Church universal.

In his speech the Pope also reiterated his oft-repeated appeals for peace and told us that he would be flying on October 4th to the United Nations headquarters in New York to deliver a message for peace. He made note of the fact that he would be making that trip in relation to the 20th anniversary of the United Nations agency and that he would be speaking for all of us bishops.

Perhaps in a veiled reference to the "bickering" that went on during the last session of the Council and the acrimony generated by the delay in bringing the religious liberty statement to vote in the last days of that session, charity formed the principle theme of the Pope's speech. "This development in charity," he said, "ought to characterize the conclusion of our Ecumenical Council . . . in our search for truth, whether doctrinal or disciplinary, let love guide us."

The Holy Father's speech before some 2,000 bishops, and hundreds of periti, priests, religious and laity brought to a close the opening plenary meeting of the fourth session of Vatican II.

Before we began to move from our places in St. Peter's Basilica, and while waiting for the Pope to begin his exit, the Secretary General advised us that the 128th General Congregation of the Council, the first of the fourth session of Vatican II, would meet the next day at nine o'clock and that the very first item on the agenda would be the proposed statement on Religious Liberty.

The Holy Father, disregarding the portable papal throne on which he was carried into St. Peter's, walked the whole length of the main aisle, stopping and waving to us bishops as applause accompanied his passage to the rear of the church.

September 22, 1965

A week ago we began our work on this session of Vatican II. After the Council Secretary got through some housekeeping details, Cardinal Tisserant, as head of the Council Presidents, assured us that there would continue to be complete freedom of speech. He urged the bishops not to repeat what was already said and he issued the usual warning against applauding. That was ignored because right after we received the papal document spelling out details of the new Synod of the world's bishop's, and the Pope was present for this, applause broke out.

As was promised us at the end of the last session, the declaration on Religious Liberty was the first matter of business. A roster of twenty-two Cardinals who would speak was announced, among them two Americans, Spellman of New York and Cushing of Boston.

I should tell you that since the last session the American bishops have been working out their own strategy for support of the declaration. Back in December, Cardinal Ritter of St. Louis sent us a letter outlining his observations and urged that we support the text given us just prior to the conclusion of the third session. Last January, Archbishop O'Boyle, President of our National Conference, sent on to us observations by several experts on that matter of

Religious Liberty.

Cardinal Spellman in his intervention, keeping in mind Ritter's suggestion, stated that, "Every man must be free from every form of coercion. The schema is not in conflict with the state and radical revision of the document as it now stands would give rise to doubts about the Council's sincerity in this field." Cardinal Cushing supported the present text by adding, "Although I am not renowned as a philosopher, I know that every right finds its foundation in truth. And religious liberty is based on truth and works for the good of society."

As usual the opposition, as was the case last year, came from the Spanish and Italian bishops who receive a great deal of support for their churches from their governments. Basically, they are not for the separation of church and state. Our own experience in the United States has taught us to be wary of state support in religious matters. The Spanish Cardinal, who spoke against the declaration, was quite direct in stating that, "Although the schema was most important because it dealt with protecting and safeguarding the faith, only the Catholic Church has the right to preach the Gospel. Therefore, proselytism in predominately Catholic countries must be suppressed, even by the state."

The Spaniard went so far as to insist that if the religious liberty document passed it would ruin the Catholic countries. To put it in a nutshell, the declaration limits itself to the problem of "human and civil rights in matters religious as indicated in present day society."

Bishop de Smet of Belgium, from whom I took that quote, presented the schema to us that morning. In giving a kind of report of the work on the document while we were in recess, he further said, "The purpose of the document is the good of the human person which is owed to him in justice, namely, that he should be free from coercion in religious matters . . . and, men today are increasingly aware that they have a right to personal independence and to responsible freedom."

And may I remind you how important this declaration is for us who are interested in ecumenism, in better relationships with our other Christian brothers and sisters, as well as non-Christians. We need to live together in freedom and know what a price we've paid for that freedom in the United States.

Last year, the very same day of our discussions, in the evening, Father John Courtney Murray, an expert in the area of religious liberty and a "peritus" of the Council, gave a conference on the day's discussion. He analyzed the interventions of the Spanish and Italian bishops and dissected their references to several Popes whom they quoted against the document. Contrarily, Father Murray showed that Pius XII, one of those Popes, heightened consciousness of the truth of the dignity of the human person in all of his teachings. And he went on to say that Pope John XXIII, in his encyclical "Peace of Earth," built on Pius XII by insisting that there is the "truth of man's endowment with natural rights and duties and the truth of the juridical nature of the state, that is, its primary duty to protect man's rights and the facilitation of the performance of these duties."

During the last session of the Council, one of the Italian cardinals made a big issue of the use of the word, "tolerance," in connection with other sects penetrating the religious life in a so-called Catholic country. I remember one of those Cardinals saying that only the Church has possession of the truth. Father Murray attacked that concept on the basis of past papal doctrine on civil tolerance as well as the teaching of the Church concerning the historic conception of what is a Catholic State.

"Tolerance," according to Murray has to do with evil and only God may be said to tolerate evil." He based this view on several passages from scripture, one of which, John 2:25, states that "God, who knows what is in man, is the judge of truth and error, good and evil. Man is not the judge of the heart of his brother."

"Tolerance," Murray went on to say, "is a moral issue which concerns men in their relation to one another in a world in which errors and evils are current, but over which the order of truth and morality holds sway. The forbidden thing is that man should call error truth and evil good."

"Tolerance" is a civil issue and here concerns government in relation to society and the schema emphasizes this. No government may lay upon its citizens a positive mandate, or give them a positive authorization, to teach or to do what is contrary to truth and morality.

And so, were there the space, I could go on citing the practical problems Father Murray brought us relative to the application of the principle of religious liberty. To cite just this one, how may the state lend financial or other assistance to the Church and facilitate the free exercise of religion in society?

September 28, 1965

I did mention to you before that the Religious Liberty schema was "our baby" in the Council. So I hope you don't mind more information on our problems with that document. And here we are, almost at the end of the month and there is so much to report to you of our daily happenings here in Rome. I'll try to be brief.

On the 16th, the second day of our debate on Religious Liberty, there was extensive disagreement over the theological basis of that document. For instance, in contrast to Cardinal Ritter's (St. Louis) strong affirmation of the schema and its theological correctness, a Spanish-born bishop from China, with apparent anger no less, insisted that the document was so fraught with error that it should be thrown out. He claimed that the minority view which spoke for the traditional teachings of the Church on Religious Liberty was being ignored.

A German Cardinal, Jaeger of Paderborn, who spoke in the name of 150 bishops, tackled the touchy problem of the privileged status for a religion in a country. He cited Italy and Spain where Catholicism is the state religion, Anglicanism in England and Lutheranism in the Scandinavian countries. His was a balanced presentation in that, he felt that although such state religions still existed (a hold-over from the Middle Ages) such a situation should not interfere with equal rights for others.

Get the point? Suppose Washington were to decide that Protestantism would be the state religion for the United States.

And so we went on. After five days of debate, on the 21st, the Council Fathers voted overwhelmingly to give the world a definitive document spelling out man's civil right to religious freedom.

That out of the way, we plunged into study, debate and consensus on the lengthy and complicated schema on the Church in the Modern World, a document that was the brainchild of Pope Paul VI when he was Archbishop of Milan, and his friend, Cardinal Suenens of Belgium.

The Archbishop of Toulouse, France, presented the schema to us and gave us this brief summary: Of its two parts, the first makes clear that the basic problem was the problem of man himself and what the Church has to say about man where his salvation will come from. The second part takes on a great deal of human society in all of its phases, marriage and family, for instance. The holiness of marriage, married love and respect for human life; the political community; peace and the community of nations, and dialogue with unbelievers.

At this point of our stay in Rome, Bishop O'Donnell and I began to miss the teaching and learning presence of Cardinal Meyer. Here we were, back in Rome, in the same rooms, advanced in our seat arrangements in St. Peter's by reason of seniority and answering questions about the

Cardinal's illness and death. Gone are the scholarly dinners on Via Sardegna and those long evenings at the feet of a master; those daily trips to St. Peter's with the Cardinal and his knowing way of reaching into his briefcase to test us with his intervention for that morning.

I do recall Cardinal Meyer, on our return home after the third session of the Council in a talk he gave our seminarians at Mundelein, epitomized the schema on the Church in the Modern World this way: "We are meeting (in Rome) to confront the Catholic Church with the modern world and to confront the modern world with the Church." And he went on to say that :

"We are all sinners. Despite Baptism we still carry the consequences of original sin. If the schema is really aimed at reaching the heart of the modern world it should emphasize that the Church is the home of the weak and the refuge of those who experience difficulties."

What he was saying came out of an intervention the Cardinal made last year when the document on the Church and the World was first introduced to us in Council in its draft form. My notes do not indicate the date, but His Eminence did say:

"The schema does say much about the different ways in which the Christian living in the world ought to work for the advancement of the temporal order." Yet, the Cardinal insisted that it does not make clear how a person's vocation in the world can be a part of our salvation. "We should not forget that God offers the hope of glory not just to man's soul, but to his whole person and to the entire world. No one denies that along the way man fairly often misuses the world and the good things that make it up."

I loved that reference to the ecology which we are destroying by our wasteful habits. Remember, in one of my talks I urged that if you have to uproot a tree on your property for some good reason, replace it with another tree elsewhere. And finally, this is how the Cardinal aimed at our consciences: "The whole world is not only the means by which redeemed man perfects himself, but is itself the object of redemption just as our bodies are."

September 30, 1965

Here, at Vatican II, for the first time, and before a gathering of the world's bishops for the fourth and final meeting of a Council of the universal Church, a Pope decided to have an advisory body with him and under him as the final teaching and decision making body in the Church.

Now we wonder what Cardinal Meyer would have said of the new Synod of Bishops and the passage of the Religious Liberty declaration.

And these days we wondered what his approach would be to schema 13 (on the Church in the Modern World) to which he referred at one time as the other pivotal document of the Council. As the shepherd of the large and busy Archdiocese of Chicago, and even before as a seminary rector, bishop of Superior, Wisconsin, and archbishop of Milwaukee, he had many opportunities to witness the alienation between the Christian Gospel he knew so well as a biblical scholar and the solution he would be offering the Council these days as we struggle for a bridge that will bring the Church to a world yearning for Christ's saving message.

A little over a week ago the revised schema on the Church in the Modern World was presented to us for study and discussion. Probably the most voluminous of the Council documents, we are eager to see how we can relate our beloved Church to its place and role in our modern times.

A number of the Council Fathers on the first day of debate objected to the fact that the schema neglects the presence of evil in the world and man's struggle with his own weaknesses as a consequence of original sin. Those speeches reminded me of that same kind of objection Cardinal Meyer voiced when we were discussing the Dogmatic Constitution on the Church. You may remember that I reported his words this way:

"In order that our schema may reach the hearts of men today, men who are burdened by a sense both of sin and of their own moral weakness, I am emboldened to propose this change: My preference is that before the People of God is described as being without stain or wrinkle, we emphasize that the Church is the household of the Father of mercies in which the failings of the prodigal sons are forgiven, their wounds are bound up, their weaknesses cured, and their needs are answered."

I'll not get into the theological debate that accompanied those early objections to the schema except to say that Cardinal Meyer's old friend, Cardinal Doepfner of Munich, Germany summed up those theological technicalities by stating that, "the consequences of sin are not sufficiently emphasized" and warned against leaving in the text a sense of false optimism. He felt that the schema runs the risk of arousing false hopes.

If I were to capsulize the thinking during those early days of debate, at least as I see it, here we were ready to tackle the modern world and the Church's relationship to the world without spelling out very directly who makes up our modern world and what are the difficulties of living in that world. What I feel faces us is the task of recognizing that man is both a spiritual and a social being living in an a-spiritual world.

My favorite bishop-speaker at the Council, Leon Elchinger of Strasbourg, France last Friday reminded us that we keep in mind the intention of Pope John XXIII in calling the Council, namely that we "show the world a renewed face of the Church that would attract all men by the splendor of Christ's teaching."

I realized when the Bishop said, "the present text says

much about what the world must do but says little about what the Church must do to come into closer contact with the world" that he was again echoing Pope John's dream of "bringing the modern world into contact with the vivifying and perennial energies of the Gospel." And that reminded me of the sentence from Pope John's diary, "We must infect the world with Christ."

I mentioned earlier the size of "schema 13," that on the Church in the Modern World. It is obvious that a great deal of study went into preparation of the document. I heard from one of the commission members that this was the twentieth version. I suspect that as the days go by there will be more discussion and more changes as we try to express the Church's relationship to the world. Consider for a moment just these headings from certain sections of the document: Solidarity of the Church With the Whole Human Family; the Service of Man; Hopes and Anxieties; Changes in the Social Order; Psychological, Moral, and Religious Changes; and then this chapter heading – The Church and the Human Condition – and that section alone encompasses subheadings like: The Vocation of the Human Person, Man in the Image of God, The Dignity of the Human Body, The Dignity of Conscience, The Grandeur of Liberty, Victory over Death, etc.

So you see what we are in for here in Rome and please understand why it would be impossible for me to report in detail on say, just half of that subject matter. I liked this observation of an archbishop from India who said:

"The work of the Council is not to sum up everything that has been written these past few years on the problems of the world; rather, it is to give a new impetus to the Church which must respond without further delay to the appeals which God addresses to her through events. The Church is often behind the times.

Are we ourselves men of our times? We monologue here day after day with speeches. Happily, there are the coffee bars where we can exchange ideas."

I think you get the archbishop's point, too many bishops are "grand-standing," looking for limelight and not sticking to the work at hand. Some say the fault is at the top, the way our meetings are conducted, and they conclude that comes of the fact that the ten presidents, who take turns chairing our sessions, and the four moderators, responsible for the agenda items, were all chosen by the Pope and not elected by the Council members. Well!

October 7, 1965

I should tell you that while I may be giving you the impression that we are sailing through the doldrums as far as all the speech making goes we are voting on the completed text of a number of documents. For instance, after more than twenty votes the Dogmatic Constitution on Divine Revelation was approved by the bishops and now waits on acceptance and promulgation by the Pope.

And then we were receiving for study the texts of amendments and observations on other documents that we would be voting on in the future, texts like that on the Role of the Laity in the Church, on Seminaries and Christian Education.

On October 1st, the Secretary announced that in the course of the morning's work, and within the week, we would be asked to cast some nineteen votes on the revised schema on Religious Life, seven votes on the Seminary Training of Priests; five votes on Christian Education and fifteen votes on the Church's Relation With Non-Christian Religions.

A week ago, an archbishop from Egypt kind of tossed a bombshell into our proceedings when discussion on the section on marriage in the schema on the Church in the Modern World came up. He asked that the Church cast a merciful eye on the plight of husbands and wives who have been abandoned, and asked: "Could not the Church dispense the innocent party from the bonds of matrimony?"

You could, as we say, cut the silence in St. Peter's that morning, with a knife – and the coffee bars were virtually abandoned as we continued the debate on marriage.

Understandably, much of our discussion here in the past week continued to dwell on the nature and end of marriage. One of the bishops, in a kind of moment of pique suggested that we "throw out the whole section on marriage because the Pope had reserved to himself the decision on its greatest problem, birth control." Most of us felt that our discussions would help the Pope make a decision on that thorny subject.

By the way, that "bombshell," tossed into our midst by the bishop who was concerned about the plight of individuals in marriages where there was desertion or mental illness continued to smolder. Several bishops continued to raise questions about the present practice of the Church in handling that type of situation and marriage separations generally. Again, most of us felt those were problems for canon lawyers who would be writing and interpreting the new laws on marriage following the Council. We continued to concentrate, therefore, on the very nature and end of marriage.

Cardinal Suenens, who, with Pope Paul VI, inspired the schema under debate, provided the setting for such discussion in these words:

"It is essential that we have a better understanding of the laws of human fecundity, for men as well as women; that we also have a better understanding of the psychological laws of self-control, and that we have a better understanding of the laws of conjugal life as a whole."

The Cardinal went on to tell us that the present theology of marriage is linked to out-of-date knowledge. Medical and psychological discoveries showing the specific character of human sexuality must be integrated into it. A number of bishops talked about the significant documents available to us from Pope Pius XII who, in one instance that I looked up here at our library, linked human sexuality with what God must have intended in the act of creating man and woman. In a talk to midwives the Pope said that:

"The same creator has also decreed that in this function of procreation the partners should experience pleasure and happiness of body and spirit. Husband and wife, therefore, by seeking and enjoying this pleasure do no wrong. They accept what the Creator has destined for them."

If I understood what Pope Pius XII was saying, he is telling us that in addition to the physical and sexual aspects, marriage has above all a spiritual dimension.

Here is one passage of several from the schema on the Church in the Modern World that I would share with you:

"Married love is an eminently human love because it is affection between two persons rooted in the will and it embraces the good of the whole person . . . it is experienced in tenderness and action, and permeates their whole lives; besides, this love is actually developed and increased by the exercise of it. This is a far cry from mere erotic attraction, which is pursued in selfishness and soon fades away in wretchedness."

Last Tuesday, the Holy Father returned from his trip to the United Nations in New York. He came directly to St. Peter's from the airport and gave us a report of his experience. You may be, because of the media coverage, familiar with his speech to that international body of nations so there is no need for my repeating what he said.

October 12, 1965

I'll get back to the document on the Church in the Modern World, but meanwhile I should tell you that we've been voting on various documents these days, the vote on the Pastoral Role of Bishops was completed and approved and will be waiting on the Holy Father's decision to promulgate that schema; we began voting on the document on the Renewal of Religious Life as well as on the schema on the Missions.

Regarding the document on Religious Life, you will be interested in knowing that an extensive change in the garb of both men and women religious is foreseen as a result of language in the schema. A vote on an amendment to the original text included the recommendation that the garb of religious be more in keeping with our modern times. I suspect that we will be seeing a change in the way our religious Sisters dress in the United States. As far as the men are concerned, the cassock here in Europe is already giving way to the clerical suit in which you are used to seeing us back home. As a matter of fact, we American bishops simply refuse to be seen shopping around Rome in cassocks.

I remember when I lived in Paris during the war years, the women used to laugh at the priests riding their bicycles with cassocks tucked above their naked knees. The same was true in Rome. It was all right for the girls to be flashing along the streets with skirts flying in every which direction, but men, well!

To my surprise, I learned from my English bishop friend and neighbor here in the Council that Pope Pius XII specifically asked religious women to update their garb. Some did, some moved slowly and some not at all. We're now convinced that the wording in the Religious Life schema will move things along in that regard.

And that vow of chastity that religious take. Well, that with the change to more modern garb, it may be harder to keep. In any case, a section in the Religious Life document states that, "psychological maturity is required for this vow, and superiors should see to it that their subjects are not allowed to take such a vow (of chastity) without this maturity." Let's see what the future will bring.

By the way, the final vote on that religious habit thing was 2,110 bishops for, 20 against.

The new draft of the document on Christian Education was given us today to study. The text emphasizes that Catholic schools avoid the attitude of "protecting children from the world, asking rather that they become apostolic schools, training children to become apostles in the world." Another interesting facet of this new text states that parents are obliged to send their children to Catholic schools "where feasible." Present canon law, which will be changed, states that parents are bound under "severe obligation" to send their children to Catholic schools.

Yesterday, Pope Paul VI informed us that he intends to maintain the ancient law of clerical celibacy and has therefore removed that subject from the competence of the Council. His letter to us stated that, "public debate on the subject is not opportune, and I intend not only to maintain the discipline but to reinforce its observance." The Pope then suggested that if any of us wished to express our views on the subject we are encouraged to write to him personally.

The only other time the Pope intervened in our work here was last year when we began early discussion of the draft on the Church in the Modern World. Then he removed discussion of birth control from the agenda in favor of his setting up a special commission to study the subject.

And here is other news that will be of interest to you. One of our American bishops, Hallinan of Atlanta, Georgia filed a statement with the Council's Secretary on changes in the Role of Women in the Church. "Since women constitute half the people of God they should," said Archbishop Hallinan, "be given equal consideration in the schema on the Church in the Modern World and every opportunity should be given them to offer their special talents to the service of the Church."

Specifically, said Archbishop Hallinan, "Women should take on certain liturgical functions in the Mass; they should be ordained deaconesses, encouraged to become teachers and consultants in theology, etc." His statement recalled that Pope Paul VI in 1961, when he was Archbishop of Milan, said that, "women must come closer to the altar, to souls and to the Church in order to gather together the people of God."

And Archbishop Hallinan's statement goes on to say that although "the Church has struggled to free women from the old place of inferiority . . . the Church has been slow in denouncing the degradation of women and in claiming for them the right of suffrage and economic equality . . . it has failed, in offering the selection of their vocations, any choice but that of mother and nun."

So much for that. As of today we have completed work on four documents and three others are in their final stages of debate. The Pope told us today that he would be joining us on October 28th at a public session at which we suspect he will promulgate those four completed schemas.

October 14, 1965

We're moving along. Today we began discussion on the last document scheduled for Council debate, that on Priestly Life and Ministry. Naturally, we bishops looked forward to discussing the life and ministry of those who are our closest collaborators.

How we wished, Bishop O'Donnell and I, that Cardinal Meyer were here to participate in the discussion of priests and the priesthood he loved so dearly. His old friend,

Cardinal Ruffini of Palermo, Italy rose to say that the schema was "worthy of high praise because it was drawn from genuine sources of piety."

I recall one of Cardinal Meyer's talks to a class of priests celebrating their anniversaries at our seminary in Mundelein. I don't have the text in front of me but shall never forget his emphasis on the priest, "the Man," whose holiness must shine forth before those whom he serves. The man, who by virtue of his ordination for a special mission, needs to be close to God.

I think I mentioned this before. The question is whether a diocesan priest can achieve the same degree of holiness as a priest belonging to a religious order. A bishop the other day said it well when he said, "The question of whether a busy diocesan priest can be said to live in a state of holiness as do religious priest is still an open one . . . but the text seems to imply that such a state is impossible for diocesan priests." Again, I would have loved to have had Cardinal Meyer's reaction to that.

And, he would have turned over in his grave had he, as did all of us here in St. Peter's, received a letter (against Council rules) asking us to reject the statement on the Jews and non-Christian religions which he espoused so strongly, if you remember. When it came to a vote the other day, that statement received 1,937 yes votes, and 153 negative ones indicating how ineffective that letter was.

And parents, you will be interested in a vote we had on an amendment to the Christian Education schema. The impression was given by the press that the Council urged governments, by a vote of 2,000 to 85, to pay subsidies to parents so that they could be free in choice of a school for their children.

Subsequent analysis of the amendment's rather unclear wording showed that was not true. Were there to be a positive move in the direction of subsidies to parents sending their children to private schools, most of us here would have preferred Cardinal Spellman's more direct wording, that there ought to be provided, "a due measure of public aid" to parents.

I did promise to get back to the document on the Church in the Modern World. Here is a brief report on that schema's contribution to culture. Understandably, the Church has always been interested in culture. Witness its dedication to the arts, to music, architecture, sculpture and the like. I'm sure you can visualize the beauty that adorns our churches if you only had the opportunity to drink in all that we enjoy here in Rome in that area – the vastness of St. Peter's, the Sistine Chapel and the gorgeous paintings of Michelangelo in its ceilings, the Vatican museum and so much here in Rome that bespeaks culture and the Church.

Our particular document, however, addresses culture in the broader sense. For instance, this Council is a cultural event, that it speaks to people of various cultures, European and non-European, the culture of black Africa, of Latin America, the Oriental cultures that go back thousands of years. It speaks of how the mission countries had, in Christianizing them, imposed on them a Western-European culture. It tackles the problem of how far adaptation to another culture can go as far as our liturgy is concerned and what is still essential to Christianity.

The sheer cultural dimension of the Council stands out as we begin to delve into the meaning of the Church and its relationship to modern man and woman. Why, just as I look around at the bishops who surround me here and count the countries from which they come, that cultural dimension of the Church is most apparent, and, there faces us the dichotomy of all those cultures as we try to define and speak of the one Church of Christ.

I think of how broad was Pope John's vision of the Church and the varying cultures that make it up. I recall that in his opening and welcoming speech in October 1962 he criticized "those prophets of doom" who, looking at our multi-cultured Church, would only forecast disaster for this one Church of Christ if the Council were to build on his dream of what our Church ought to be for the men and women of our time. This is a quote from that talk:

"In the present order of things, Divine Providence is leading us to a new order of human relations which . . . despite our human differences lead to the greater good of the Church."

I think also that I had a keener appreciation of what Pope John was striving for as a result of my worldside travels on behalf of our American bishops' relief and rehabilitation agency, Catholic Relief Services, with which I was associated for sixteen years. As one of its three founders, I relished the rich tapestry of a world-wide church that worshiped the One God in different languages and in different ways.

How sweet for me, therefore, were Pope John's words. "The substance of the ancient doctrine of the deposit of faith is one thing, and the way in which it is presented is another."

October 19, 1965

I am fascinated by this section of the schema on the Church in the Modern World and its hopes for contribution to culture. I can't help but think of how, prior to this Council, the cultural makeup of our Church was virtually ignored in the theological formation I received in the seminary. As a matter of fact, I was given the impression that the "world" and the culture that existed outside the seminary gates was bad. Contact with that world and that culture would be the ruination of my priestly vocation. This schema 13, more formally the schema of the Church in the Modern World, promises to open new vistas toward the world.

Pope Paul VI, who was a potent force behind the schema 13 when he was Archbishop of Milan, Italy, reminded us in his speech at the opening of the second session of the Council in 1963, that the Church must not "close in on itself and place itself between Christ and the world . . . it will need to build a bridge toward the contemporary world, "and let it know that, the Church looks at it with profound understanding, with sincere admiration and with the sincere intention not of conquering it, but of serving it; not of despising it, but of appreciating it; not of condemning it, but of strengthening and saving it."

I think I mentioned this in one of my earlier letters, but the world I'm again discovering here by the presence of the bishops from every part of our planet is a world of different mentalities and cultures, Asian, Black African, European, North American, Latin American, a plurality of minds expressing the diversity that makes us the One, Holy, Catholic, and Apostolic, yet universal Church.

But besides the bishops, there were, as you know, those periti whom they brought with them. Theologians, scripture scholars, liturgy people and other experts whose specific expertise and contribution to the writings of the Council was often colored by the culture from which they came. That is why future historians will be able to read into the documents of Vatican II the cultural influence of our contemporary world and understand why, for instance, when we discussed the language of the Mass, we moved to adaptation.

A remarkable byproduct of Vatican II will be a vision of the church aware of its cultural diversities, linked with Rome, but eager to flex its muscles in order to meet the particular needs of a particular people of God whom it has been called to serve. The local Church will never be the same again.

I should tell you that the Pope has decided to give us a week's recess in order to give the various commissions time to rewrite the draft documents on which we voted. We've a suspicion that when we meet again the Holy

Father will be announcing his approval and promulgation of some on those completed documents.

What will we do with all that time? I hear bishops, especially those who live in Europe are having a chance to get back to their dioceses; others, especially Americans, will be heading for brief vacations in the Holy Land. The shrines at Lourdes and Fatima are on some schedules. I noticed that when we voted on one of the completed documents the other day, the number of votes was down to 1521, a sign that some of the bishops have already begun that recess.

As for me, there will be a golf game or two and some side trips to Florence, Venice, and as one of our bishops proposes, a drive to the warmer beaches and villas of southern Italy. A lot of us are aware of the fact that this is the last session of the Council and perhaps our last chance to get around Europe again.

October 26, 1965

After that week-long recess, we are now ready to face up to the conclusions on several schemas, on Priestly Life and Ministry and the revised text on Religious Liberty. A number of speakers made strong pleas for the redistribution of priests. In a "priest poor" region, one man may have to serve 25,000 souls, whereas in other places, like the United States, there may be one priest for just 1,500 Catholics.

An important observation was made by one bishop relative to the nature of the duties performed by the modern day priest. I suspect the bishop had in mind our document on the Church in which we called for a wider involvement of the laity in the work and mission of the Church. Citing the "dramatic evolution of the modern world," that bishop urged "a balance between ordinary priestly duties and those which laity could easily perform." Here, I feel, the liturgy document that was promulgated in December, 1963 will provide good examples of various roles that the laity can take over in the liturgy of the Mass. The restored order of the permanent diaconate will also relieve priests of certain duties, like wake services, marriage preparation programs, etc.

I am also thinking of the many positions that lay persons have already and will assume to relieve the parish priests of tasks they can better fulfill; secretarial work, bookkeeping, accounting, property management, areas of work for which priests are not trained in the seminary.

As a matter of fact, there will be new administrative procedures that will involve not only the parish office and rectory, but the bishop's office and chancery as well. Much has been written into the Council documents that will literally change the face of the Church.

The other evening I went to a lecture at which a Jesuit priest from France presented some worrisome problems about the future of the priesthood. He spoke of a "crisis" in the priesthood, of a vocation shortage, of how our seminaries are being depleted, and that "celibacy is becoming the subject of conversation in circles where it was never mentioned before." And then he went on to say something that reminded me of our discussions on the place of the Church in the Modern World. He said, "now that the sacral society has dissolved (I thought that was too strong a word) and given way to a technological and secular society, a crisis has emerged that cannot be remedied." Really, that sounded to me like we bishops here at the Council were blind to the situation of the Church in the world, its lack of influence and our "hopes and desires" to turn the world toward Christ. I hope that priest is not a prophet.

I should mention that yesterday evening the American bishops here held a meeting at their college here to discuss the ramifications of a document we discussed and voted on regarding the Pastoral Office of Bishops that had particular reference to national conferences of bishops, something much too technical for your interest. I bring the matter up only to tell you that last year our Cardinal Meyer was chosen chairman of a special committee that would study the implications of that document on our National Conference of Catholic Bishops. Last evening, Cardinal Krol of Philadelphia was chosen to replace Cardinal Meyer.

As for the Religious Liberty schema, the bishop, who introduced it to us for discussion, stated that the new text puts "greater emphasis on the Church's teaching, that the right to religious liberty does not free the individual or society from the moral obligation of finding and following the true faith." And that bishop went on further to remind us that, "the foundation for religious liberty is to be found in the Catholic teaching on the dignity of the human person."

It's now certain that when we meet with the Holy Father on Thursday, the 28th, five completed documents will be promulgated by the Pope. On November 18th, we're told, six more documents will be published and in order to give our special committees time to prepare those final texts, we'll be given another recess, from October 30th to November 8th.

November 9, 1965

We're back at work again. Given the target date of December 8th for the conclusion of this fourth and last session of Vatican II, we are just beyond the half way point of our meetings. By the way, our debates or discussions, if you will, have come to an end, and our principle activity these days involves study and voting on the completed documents. Admittedly, things are getting a bit boring but I'll still have more to report to you. One of the bishops here is quoted as saying, "There are no surprises anymore, so let's go home."

So where are we? The completed schema on Religious Liberty has been given us and we now await the final vote on that interesting and controversial document. I'm betting RL, as we here affectionately refer to it, will get through this time despite what some say will be a small pocket of opposition. The thorny problem of the relationship between Scripture and Tradition is still holding up the schema on Divine Revelation. I think that Cardinal Meyer would be exasperated with the delay.

In the works, as we would put it back home, are the schemas on the Missions, Priestly Life and the still unsatisfactory text on the Church in the Modern World. Imagine, there are 25 sub-commissions working on that document and they promise us that a completed text for our review might be available in a week or so.

You know, a lot of us bishops here feel that all of that work, all of those documents, all of our hopes will depend in large measure on the implementation of those texts as instruments of the Church's renewal. Twenty-five or fifty years from now, I wonder if the forces here that have blocked so much of the Council's energies will rise up again to push the Church back to look in on herself with consequent neglect of the world she has been asked to serve and communicate with.

Being here and watching "the opposition" work – those who want to hold on to the status quo – has been an education to me. I really worry about what will happen after we bishops go back home, plunge into meeting the needs of our local churches, and the old guard stays here to maneuver the future.

It could be that if the Synod of Bishops really works out, the bishops meeting periodically with the Pope, Vatican II and its documents may live in the years to come. A report I've read here states that the Synod may "actually be an extended council." I hope and pray for that.

October 28th was a banner day for us. Pope Paul VI joined us for Mass and later approved and officially promulgated five of the Council documents. You might be interested in that part of the ceremony.

Before Mass started, the Council Secretary stood next to the Pope and read the first and last phrases of each document. He then asked us to mark a kind of IBM ballot in either the affirmative of negative. During Mass the votes were counted and at its conclusion the Secretary announced the results. There was applause after each of these announcements. And then came the formal promulgation by the Pope; one formula that covered all five of the documents. Parts of it went this way, "The decrees and declarations read in brief before this Second Vatican Council, lawfully assembled, I now decree and enact them and command that what has been thus enacted be promulgated for the glory of God."

Those five documents the Pope, with the help of his bishops gave to the Church, will have a profound impact upon your daily lives as Catholics if they are clearly implemented. Those documents lay down principles rather than norms and herein lies the difficulty with implementing them. Catholics for generations have become used to laws and regulations, being told what to do. Now, as some parts of those documents imply, you will have to form your own conscience based on your understanding of those principles.

Let's take an example: Confession. After you have confessed your sins, the priest may turn to you and say, "Now you decide what kind of penance you deserve for those sins. After all, you are in the best position to judge how grievously you have offended God."

Last weekend Pope Paul VI directed an exhortation to his brother bishops related to the proximate ending of this last session of Vatican II. Because I feel that exhortation has portents for the future, I'll quote just this bit of it:

"The successful results of the Council and its salutary effects on the life of Church will depend not so much on the multiplicity of rules as on the thoroughness and zeal when putting into the practice, in the years to come, the decisions that have been issued. It will be imperative to prepare the hearts of the faithful to accept the new rulings; shaking the apathy of those who are too reluctant to adapt themselves to the new order, and restraining the zeal of the others who might exaggerate their personal feeling and thus endanger the sound renewal that was undertaken."

The ever present Italian Vespas, a motorized version of a kind of bicycle with their loud exhaust systems as they make the comer here from the via Pompei onto our via Sardegna, are trying hard to divert me from completing this report of an exciting day. This morning the Holy Father, after we voted approval, promulgated the Constitution on Divine Revelation and the Decree on the Lay Apostolate.

History was made with that decree on the Role of the Laity in the Church and I look forward to implementing its directives as soon as I get back home. Here are two very strong sentences from that decree:

"The union of the Church and its members is so compact that the member who fails to make the proper contribution to the development of the Church must be said to be useful neither to the Church nor to himself. The laity must take up the renewal of the temporal order as their special obligation."

That sentence, "the union of the Church and its members is so compact," implies some very practical consequences. It de-emphasizes and tends to put an end to the "clericalization" of the Church. The Church and its mission is the affair of all Christians. We are all co-responsible for the Church and her destiny and all of us will have to render an account for the success or failure of the Church's mission on earth.

Just the titles of the various sections of that document indicate the Role of the Laity and Council had in mind: The Apostolate of Evangelization and Sanctification; The

Renewal of the Temporal Order; Charitable Works and Social Aid.

How I wished Cardinal Meyer were here this morning to witness the final vote, 2,344 to 6, of the Council Fathers on the document on Divine Revelation. I do believe that this schema on Revelation will turn out to be the most important theological text of the whole Council. It touches upon the sources of our faith and makes clear that both the written word (scripture) and the spoken word (tradition) are incontestable ways in which God reveals Himself to us. Both of those sources emerge from the same wellspring, and at certain times and in certain ways merge into one. In a way then, scripture and tradition reinforce each other. And so it was that the Council, after long and hard debate, concluded that both of these form one sacred deposit of the Word of God through which God continues to reveal himself to us.

Tomorrow, we were informed by the General Secretary, we will be asked to cast our final vote on the schema on Religious Liberty. Word is out that the document should receive a very favorable and positive vote. A favorable vote will mark the anniversary of one year and the very hour in which great disappointment reigned in the Council when its presidents decided to hold up an earlier vote that raised the ire of our late departed Cardinal Meyer. I reported the incidents of that day to you in an earlier letter.

November 30, 1965

The weather continues to be nice here in Rome. It has cooled off a bit and the evenings tend to get uncomfortable. They tell us that we will not be having heat in our temporary home for some time. Even so, we'll be on our way home in ten days or so.

I should tell you that we've been having another one of those mini-vacations, until today. With the closing of the

Council on December 8th, that means we'll be having just three or four more general meetings.

Schema 13, that on the Church in the Modern World, has been occupying our attention. Bishop McGrath of Panama, who was responsible for presenting the amended text to us, reported that over 3,000 amendments were submitted. To mention just a few: The suggestion that the document contain some statement on the possession or accumulation of nuclear weapons was dropped because the matter was beyond our competence. Regarding the documents treatment of marriage, it was decided by the commission that the Pope's decision last year to form a special group to study the birth control problem, "released the Council" from pursuing the subject.

At a press conference I attended the other day, several theologians made it clear, that, despite the Holy Father's admonition that we not touch the whole area of contraception, "theologians are free to discuss the problem in private and in theory with the hope of convincing the Church to provide some direction to that knotty problem." They seem to base their feeling on a statement the Pope made to that commission he himself had set up, namely: "All avenues are open for your investigation."

Well and good, but I have the feeling that it will be impossible to keep from public view such "private and theoretical discussions." Theory and practice are birds of a different feather. One of our American bishops, and a good friend of mine from California, stated at that conference that "theologians will continue to argue and teach privately according to their convictions on contraception." Such "teachings" always have a way of leaking out. It will be interesting what comes to us for vote on this matter of marriage and its obligations when the revised text on the Church in the Modern World is presented us.

On the question on women's role in the Church that same Bishop McGrath reported that his commission is discussing that question "as one of the signs of the time." I'm thinking of what the implications are of that statement. Certainly the presence of women here at the Council is clear indication of the Church's new attitude toward those of the faithful who constitute more than fifty percent of the Church's membership.

December 6, 1965

Today, the last working meeting day of the Second Vatican Council witnessed the presence of 2,373 bishops who voted approval of a document that puts the seal on the Church's spiritual involvement with the problems of our modern world. Maybe you are intrigued with that state-

St. Peter's Basilica, on the last working day of the Second Vatican Council, with 2,373 bishops present.

ment, that at long last, the Church is becoming interested in the world in which you especially must work out your salvation. It all comes of Pope John's dream when he asked us bishops at the opening of Vatican II in 1962 that we not look inward on ourselves, inward on the Church, but outward to that world which will which will pass us by unless we infuse into it the message of the gospels.

Meanwhile, here in Rome, the euphoria that pervades the completion of what we bishops feel was a work well done is felt everywhere. Except for the official closing ceremonies on Wednesday, Vatican II is over. Bishops are anticipating their return to their homes. There are the goodbyes and promises to keep in touch. I am thinking that after we settle in on our work back home, that promise to keep in touch will be relegated to a Christmas card for a few years.

But there will be exceptions with those whom I knew before we gathered for these historical meetings of Vatican II, bishops especially from the Third World countries, whom I was able to help through my work with Catholic Relief Services. I have no doubt that their appeals for further help will not be confined to a Christmas greeting card.

As we gather up our papers here and share those sincere feelings of departure, as far as I can tell, three attitudes emerge: Christian love, understanding and creativity.

Among us bishops and among those whom we serve, Vatican Council II has rekindled a spirit of genuine Christian love. Pope John, who gave birth to that Council, was the personal embodiment of that love and we hope that we have caught his spirit. He impressed upon us the need for that Christ-like spirit of outgoing, far-reaching love becoming a reality because we rubbed elbows with Christians from all parts on the world.

As we said our good-byes, we assured each other of a new understanding of Church. We knew that we could no longer be satisfied with the "status quo." We learned that we could no longer settle for the legalistic, regimentalized and limited view of Catholicism that we inherited from the past.

And, we learned that creativity was born of dialogue and the Council wove it into a new context. For instance, we'll be helping the Pope administer the Church through an international Synod of Bishops because a network of national and regional conferences of bishops set across the world will provide pastoral direction for that Synod just as the clergy, through a senate or presbyterial council, the laity, through parish and diocesan councils, will assist the bishop in the governance of his diocese.

And finally, Pope John's dream of a Council of unity will be perpetuated through a Secretariat for Promoting Christian unity, bringing closer together, through dialogue, those who are our brothers and sisters in Christ.

December 8, 1965

Yesterday Pope Paul VI, at what is now history, declared the final plenary meeting of Vatican II to be closed, and emphasized that "this historic assembly of the world's bishops has been deeply committed to the study and service of the modern world." And yesterday, at long last, the Pope promulgated the completed texts on Religious Liberty, on the Missions, on Priestly Life and Ministry and the Constitution on the Church in the Modern World.

This morning the Second Ecumenical Vatican Council was officially closed with a special solemn ceremony in St. Peter's Piazza. This marked the end of the Council which had been in session since October 11, 1962, a span of almost thirty-eight months. During that long period, we bishops met in 168 General Congregations or meetings. Given that figure and with the addition of ten solemn public sessions, the Council Fathers gave 615 hours to Council deliberations or the equivalent of approximately 77 eight-hour working days.

And there was that moment last September, when, confronted with the volume of material that still awaited our study and decision, most of us felt that another and fifth session and many more hours of work lay ahead. The word "impossible" dogged those early days of the fourth and promised (by the Pope) last session of Vatican II. But thanks to the careful organization by the Council Secretariat and the cooperation of the bishops, we reached this day.

This morning around 10:30 a.m. the Council Fathers gathered in their regular council seats, many wearing the gold rings given them by the Pope a few days earlier to commemorate the Council's closing. The rings, in the shape of a mitre, bear the images of Christ, Peter and Paul. Vested in cope and mitre, the bishops waited for the signal to march out the front doors of St. Peter's into the great square surrounded by the famous Bernini columns where the closing Mass of Vatican II would be celebrated.

Surrounded by his bishops, the diplomatic corps and other distinguished visitors, the Pope delivered a closing address and blessed a foundation stone which will be placed in the walls of a church to be built in commemoration of the Council. In declaring the Council of Vatican II closed, the Pope also stated that this gathering of the world's bishops "must be numbered without doubt among the greatest events of the Church. In fact it was the largest in the number of Fathers who came to the seat of Peter from every part of the world. It was the richest because of the questions which for four sessions have been discussed carefully and profoundly."

Long will I remember one of the petitions at the Offertory of the closing Mass. I sense the emotion in the Holy Father's voice when he prayed:

"That the fruits which God had deigned to bestow on his Church through this ecumenical council may be studiously grasped with sincere and open minds by all of us, we

235

beseech you hear us, O Lord."

At the end of Mass, the Council Secretary, Archbishop Felici, whom I mentioned many times in the course of these reports to you, read the official document proclaiming the closing of the Council. Then bishops, special guests and thousands of priests, brothers, nuns, seminarians and laity joined in the responses to the prayers which followed. The Pope gave his apostolic blessing and suddenly it was over; the Second Vatican Ecumenical Council was history.

December 15, 1965

Now that I'm home at my familiar desk, there is this I would like to report to you of the closing of Vatican II before we plunge into preparation for the Christmas holidays.

There is for me, and I suspect many bishops who were part of the work of Vatican II, a nostalgia as we approach the end of this year of 1965. Nostalgia for Pope John XXIII who not only convened the Council but showed us how to open our hearts to each other and the world. There were, and still are, many theories about the reason why Pope John called for a council of the universal Church. But as I look back, his dream, if that be it, took on reality when the Council embraced the Pope's call for "aggiornamento," and made real the renewal of the Church in the language of our contemporary world.

And there is memory also of Pope Paul VI who so valiantly followed in thought and proposed his predecessor and brought to fitting closure what may be one of the most historic events of Church history. There is memory of how he reached out into the world with his visit to the United Nations last October, and his participation in the International Eucharistic Congress in Bombay, India in 1964.

The more time passes the better, I hope, will we see the

work of the Holy Spirit in those many documents that have come to us out of Vatican II, the more we will see that the bishops were very concerned with seeking out new truths and searching for new ways to serve humanity. Not everyone, just as many of us bishops, will be happy about certain of what might be called the "failures" of the Council. I have in mind the weaknesses of the texts on the priesthood, and priestly life and ministry; our failure, for instance, to face up to what may become a serious shortage of vocations to the priesthood and religious life.

That whole area of marriage and married life held up the document of the Church in the Modern World. We failed, I feel, to provide clear language in that matter of birth control. Would we have successfully moved toward a solution of the problem and Pope Paul given us a free hand to tackle the subject? Who knows.

Mixed marriages, dissertion on the part of one partner and the possibility of remarriage were areas we may have glossed over.

And there are so many other disappointments or failures if you want it so. As the winter months move in on us, I am leaving to another time, within the context of review and some conclusions, further explanation of what constituted the success and failures of Vatican Council II.

Looking Back and Some Conclusions

January 4, 1966 - January 29, 1966

January 4, 1966

It all began on January 25, 1959, in the historic setting of one of Rome's four major basilicas, St. Paul's Outside the Walls. There Pope John XXIII, toward the end of an amiable discourse on the theme of the day, the feast of the conversion on St. Paul, made a startling announcement. He told eighteen Cardinals that he would be arranging, according to law, a long overdue Synod of Rome for the enactment of reforms and appropriate legislation for the Diocese of Rome.

But coupled to that statement, and almost casually, he announced that he would also summon together the world's bishops for an Ecumenical Council of the universal Church.

In Rome itself and in the more conservative circles of the Church, the reaction to that statement was anything but enthusiastic. Many of the curial or office people at the Vatican saw no reason for a Council. They felt that the Church was doing quite well and besides, it would be expensive and only allow the dissatisfied members of the Church an opportunity to stir up controversy.

But Pope John, whom I got to know when he was the Vatican representative in France, in his lovable way and based on his experience as a papal diplomat, brushed aside those objections. He was, I know, intimately alive to the basic needs of religion in our times and was willing to take chances in order to put religion in a posture of primacy over the unbelief that pervaded the world.

Outside Rome, the announcement of the Council was greeted with instant applause. Many of us were familiar with the work being done in liturgy, in catechetical and scripture studies. In those areas we began to sense a real discovery of the Word of God as a living force, a growing awareness of the vital need for a dynamic, comprehensible liturgy and a realization that our methods of religious formation needed a thorough overhaul. We saw the Council as a means of bringing to light much of the positive progress made in those areas over the past twenty or more years.

So it was that we bishops made our plans to go to Rome and those with whom I talked had mingled feelings of hope and possible disillusionment. Hope, because we were intrigued with the person of Pope John and the breath of fresh air he was bringing into the Church. Fear of disappointment because of what we knew of the intransigent members of the Curia in Rome who had the inside track in the day to day workings of the Church.

My earlier letters to you described the atmosphere of those first days in Rome in 1962, so there is no need to repeat the euphoria that dominated that gathering of bishops from all over the world during the first session of Vatican II.

The tragedy of the illness of Pope John and his death cast its shadow over the interval between the first and second sessions of the Council but we were buoyant with the selection of his successor, Pope Paul.

It was commonly agreed among us bishops that if the first session was formative, the second and third sessions were definitive. It was out of those debates during those sessions that the basic purpose of the Council was clarified especially where we discussed the Nature of the Church, the relationship of the Pope and hierarchy, the re-thinking of the mission of the Church and the problem of religious liberty.

Pope Paul VI, like us, had to find his way but in the end he emerged as a sure guide and counselor.

The fourth and final session was largely in the nature of a wrap-up, an ultimate review. The more than one hundred chapters originally proposed to us had been reduced to sixteen schemata, issued either as Constitutions, Instructions, or Decrees. All in all, the four years work fulfilled Pope John's desire for a pre-eminently pastoral Council in theme and in spirit. When on December 8, 1965, Pope Paul VI declared the Council closed and sent us bishops home with his thanks and blessing, it was with a warm feeling that the original vision had not only been fulfilled, but fulfilled beyond expectations. We were convinced that the Holy Spirit was with us from the call to Council to its completion.

January 11, 1966

Vatican II had four far-reaching objectives: To develop with some precision an idea of Church, to bring about a renewal of the Church in the light of the times, to search out the way for unity among all Christians, and to open the Church to the modern world through dialogue.

We are already witnessing the results of some of those objectives. Catholic renewal is taking many forms. Some of those forms, such as the revision of the liturgy, the way in which we pray and worship, are instantly recognizable; others, that idea of Church, like the relationship between clergy and the new role of the laity and that mutual sense of mission will take time to develop.

Collegiality, dialogue, if you wish, or shared responsibility has taken on a clearly positive approach in the way we relate to each other. Bishops now share the supreme authority with and under the Pope to govern the Church and expound its teachings. They are co-responsible for the Church with the Pope.

But that renewal Pope John called for penetrates deeper than the merely organizational. Simply by drawing the bishops together, bishops and priests and laity together, the Council has quickened the feeling among many Catholics of the Church as the family of God. It has also provided a whole new theology of community, of understanding the mission of the Church.

The idea of a layperson as an apostle of Christ sounds strange to our ears today, yet, the idea that laity can be theologically equipped for a responsible role in the Church is not far-fetched at all. That a layperson can be a better advisor in secular matters is taken for granted, but as a partner in a religious cause is not a dream. After all, that is the meaning of the phrase "the priesthood of the laity," which we bishops often used in the conciliar document on the Church.

Of the many facets of Pope John's aggiornamento, the modernization of the Church, none is more compelling and an index of the future than how we are going to handle the new doctrines for new world problems. The Church has no intention of conforming to the world, but it will be examining world problems – peace, poverty, population growth, family relations and writing new doctrines about them.

And there's the drama of our desire for Christian unity. How to handle the divisions that exist among us? How to handle the loss of Catholics who reject Christianity because the Church within its ranks does not practice the love it professes? Protestant-Catholic relationships will grow for the better when the priest attracts attention because he is seen in the company of a Protestant minister. And Protestants will begin to look at their own stance. A minister friend of mine told me that his church needs an aggiornamento too!

Before I end this letter there is something I would like to say about that word "renewal" which was at the heart of Vatican II.

Renewal means a change for the better within something that exists. Both elements are necessary, something which does not and cannot change, and a quality that does change for the better.

Away back in 1962, when Pope John called his bishops to Rome for consultation, he gave us a hint at the true meaning of what he meant by "renewal." In his opening speech he made the distinction between the content of our faith and the way in which it was to be expressed to meet the needs of our time.

January 20, 1966

Last week I indicated that a new image of the Church was emerging slowly, a new world Church that was very real in that gathering of the World's bishops at Vatican II. At the Council was an eminent theologian, Father Karl Rahner, who described it as "the Church's first official self-actualization as a world Church."

When I first heard Father Rahner in Rome speaking of a "world Church," I, like probably your good selves, asked the obvious question, "But is not the Catholic Church a world Church?" I remember Father Rahner answering: "Yes, in potency, and that goes back to how we understand the world-mission of the Church as it was born of European and American colonialism, or better still, Western-European colonialism."

What Father Rahner was trying to tell us was that for centuries Europe was exporting a religion, as it did its culture and civilization, as something special, disregarding local customs and their effectiveness in proclaiming the faith. What we witnessed at the Council was a world Church acting through the reciprocal influence exercised

242

by bishops who represented their local churches. Bishops who, during the very first meeting of the Council, rejected the centralized bureaucracy of the Roman Curia which felt that it knows best what is good for the salvation of souls throughout the world.

Perhaps this example will help your understanding what Father Rahner foresees as a developing world Church. At Vatican I, a hundred years before Vatican II, bishops from Asia and Africa were present, but they were missionary bishops from Europe and America. At Vatican II we rubbed shoulders with native African black bishops and Asian bishops who represented a culture much older than our own.

At Vatican II we had a gathering of bishops acting with the Pope and under him as the final teaching and decision-making body of the Church. For the first time, non-Western bishops exercised their influence and introduced something of their customs and their way of worshiping Christ in the morning liturgies they shared with us.

Again, the best example of this that I can share with you is the enthusiasm that greeted our decision to use the vernacular languages of the world in the Mass. Latin, as you well know, had been the common cultural language for Western civilization and for that reason became the liturgical language of the Church. Latin, after Vatican II, could never again be the liturgical language of a world Church.

This simple example also demonstrates the new problems of a world Church whose non-European local churches, despite their loyalty to Rome, will find it difficult to submit to a European mentality.

Father Rahner again provided his listeners in Rome with this historical fact. "Only once before was there that transition from a regional or national to a world Church when the Church changed from a Church of the Jews to a Church of the Gentiles."

All this is said not to give the impression that a radical

change awaits the future of our Church but to emphasize, as Father Rahner does, that the "potency for a world Church" is there. After all Western culture still dominates in the world and Christianity may still be well received throughout the world as a Western export wherever it coincides with the questionable blessings of our West. And you know how widely we are imitated.

My worry is over the poverty of our witness. My world travels revealed to me the weaknesses of our faith as compared to those who enjoyed less of the world's wealth. As immigrants, our roots are Western and European, and I would like to believe that they were strong roots, well fertilized by those who nourished our faith. The worry is in the way we practice that faith today and the way we witness that faith to the world.

Father Rahner in his talk raised another question, one similar to the differences that will exist in the celebration of the liturgy. "How can a unity of faith be maintained when you have so many different religious practices? "

I think that many of us bishops at the Council, when we cast a positive vote for the vernacular, prayed silently that the Spirit would guide the Church and ourselves in the answer to that question.

January 29, 1966

Vatican II for me was not just a great heap of documents to be studied and debated, but a learning experience I shall never forget. More than that, it was a special celebration of Catholicity. I saw and I heard a Catholicism that confirmed, by earlier experience with Catholic Relief Services in various parts of the world, a Catholicism far more culturally and theologically different than one could imagine.

Through a more profound study of the central and monumental document on the Nature of our Church, I was moved to search out even more zealously the foundations of my faith. I gained new insights into the meaning of the scriptural phrase that we are together a People of God, that together we share the priesthood of Christ, and that together we are responsible for the mission of the Church on earth. How we will work out the potential of that mission remains to be seen.

Another study of the Conciliar schema known as Schema XIII, that on the Church in the Modern World, provided me with a deeper comprehension of the major problems of life today, problems that challenge the Church, even religion itself. In part, these problems are summarized and dealt with in that document. It is neither taxative nor exhaustive; it does not attempt to say everything that can be said on the subject of social justice, marriage and family, war in an atomic age, and the responsibilities of peace; but it is a broad blueprint, at least for me, of something I helped shape. What remains now for me and so many of us who are veterans of Vatican 1I, is to preach in season and out of season, the Council's determination to try to solve those problems.

Even this soon after the Council, it is impossible to exaggerate the effect Vatican II has had on the life and thinking of the Church. Even had far less been accomplished in the way of doctrinal clarification, liturgical reform, and pastoral renewal, the very fact that bishops from all parts of the world were able to get together, to exchange viewpoints and experiences, and to learn from one another, enriched the whole body of the Church.

Now time will be needed to meditate on what we bishops saw and learned, time to ponder the collective wisdom that was poured into those sixteen documents of Vatican II, time to bring all of you abreast of the Council and its meaning in your lives. Frankly, if we are to catch up with Pope John's desire for an aggiornamento, all of us, bishops, priests, religious, and laity will need to do some sprinting to catch up with the Church of Vatican II.

But really, when you look back, the changes envisaged by the Council in the ordinary life of the Church are not by any means spectacular. Even that important concept of "collegiality" or the co-responsibility of all Christians in the mission of the Church is not that new. That central theme of the Council is reflected in so many ways that we are Church, in Baptism, in the Eucharist, in the fraternal cooperation that exists between bishops, priests and the people, in the apostolic role that laity have over the centuries exercised in the Church, in what the Council emphasized as the priesthood of the faithful.

Then again that central theme of shared accountability ought to be familiar to us living in this modern world despite the fact that all around us we witness the growing desire of all people to direct their own lives. The Council brought to life heightened awareness of something that affects all our lives and that we cannot solely act on our own.

Like I said, the principal changes made by the Council are actually not that spectacular. The wider use of the vernacular languages in the Mass and sacraments will not only have world-shaking impact but a more basic and more profound intended effect to return to the sources of our faith, to Sacred Scripture and Tradition.

Our pastoral preoccupation throughout all those four years in Rome was toward the long-term and not a flash-in-the-pan desire to gain popular attention. The media manufactured the flash while we pondered the future. Come to think of it, the broadening apostolic concern of the Council to bring the laity into closer contact with the hierarchy and its work, and the acceptance of responsibility as well as privilege, are the work of years, not of days.